CHRISTIAN FASHION
IN THE TEACHING OF THE CHURCH

Introduction by
VIRGINIA CODA NUNZIANTE

CALX MARIAE
PUBLISHING

Original title: *La moda cristiana nell'insegnamento della Chiesa*
© 2022 Edizioni Fiducia, Rome, Italy

Translated by Brendan Young

Scripture quotations are from the Douay-Rheims Bible.

© 2022 Voice of the Family, Calx Mariae Publishing

Calx Mariae Publishing is an imprint of Voice of the Family, London, United Kingdom.

All rights reserved.

ISBN: 978-1-8384785-5-1

www.voiceofthefamily.com

CONTENTS

Introduction   9

The Teaching of the Popes from Benedict XV to Pius XII

        Benedict XV   42

        Pius XI   50

        Pius XII   56

The Teaching of Two Cardinals   97

Introduction

1. WHAT IS FASHION?

Moral tracts and manuals of the Church's social teaching (which constitutes a branch of her morality) often ignore or neglect the question of Christian fashion, which has important implications both on an individual and social level.

To examine this topic in depth, we offer a selection of teachings from the popes of the twentieth century, especially Venerable Pius XII (1939–1958). On our part, we limit ourselves to a few general considerations.

The meaning of the term "fashion" is derived from that of the Latin *modus* which means "manner, norm, rule, measure". Only in the sixteenth century did the French term *mode* take on a new meaning, translated into English as "fashion".[1]

When we speak about fashion, we generally refer to clothing, especially women's clothing, but the word and concept cover innumerable manifestations of human activity: artistic and literary forms, social attitudes and ways of thinking reflected in public opinion. So-called "political correctness" can be defined as an expression of the prevailing intellectual fashion. The *Grande Dizionario della Lingua Italiana* defines "fashion" (*moda*) as a "current of thought, philosophical, ideological, artistic or literary direction or movement, which prevails in the trend of a specific period and represents, in general opinion, the

---

[1] The Oxford English Dictionary, Clarendon Press, Oxford 1939, Vol. IX, p. 939.

maximum novelty, sophistication, topicality, innovation — mostly independently of the real cultural value (often with a negative connotation, due to the superficial, empty and purely aesthetic purpose which determines its composition and success)".[2]

The negative opinion of fashion to which the dictionary refers, derives from the fickleness that is generally attributed to it. Fashion differs from customs, usage, or tradition because it is characterised by changeability and not by permanence. The customs of a people are, in this respect, the opposite of fashion, because fashion is changeable, whilst customs endure over time. Customs are the habitual usage of a region or nation — its natural aspects, analogous to its language and landscape — whilst fashion has the tendency to break up the customs and traditions of peoples. Customs can be lost but their memory remains over time. Fashion, on the other hand, does not evoke memories or nostalgia but is fleeting by its very nature. As has been noted, its fundamental essence is change.[3]

Following fashion, therefore, means following something changing without ever reaching it, believing that the passage of time dictates the rules of thinking and dressing. The title of a work by Gilles Lipovetsky, *The Empire of the Ephemeral*,[4]

---

[2] Salvatore Battaglia, article *Moda*, *Grande Dizionario della Lingua italiana*, Utet, Torino, 1978, republished in 2004, Vol. X, p. 637.

[3] Yuniya Kawamura, *La Moda*, il Mulino, Bologna 2018, p. 12.

[4] Gilles Lipovetsky, *L'empire de l'éphémère. La mode et son destin dans les sociétés modernes*, Gallimard, Paris 1987. The English translation is titled *The Empire of Fashion: Dressing Modern Democracy*.

expresses it well. "Our fashion-society," he says, "has definitively liquidated the power of the past which was embodied in the universe of tradition ... the present has become the main axis of social duration."[5]

Lipovetsky traces the birth of fashion, as we know it today, back to the mid-nineteenth century and defines it as a democratic revolution, developed homogeneously until the 1960s. *Haute couture* ("high fashion"), created and developed in nineteenth-century France, as the industry of luxury *par excellence*, actually contributed to launching the democratisation and standardisation of ways of dressing. The development of industrial sewing would cause not only the disappearance of countless regional folk costumes, but also of the differences in clothing between the classes. The desire for "fashion", the taste for novelty, the valuing of certain frivolities, once reserved for the elite, expanded and "democratically" made ways of dressing more alike. The role of "fashion creators" is intimately connected with the egalitarian ideal which fashion manifests.

Lipovetsky's book also dispels some of the misconceptions, which accompany the idea of fashion. One of these is that fashion is born from a desire for spontaneity and freedom. In reality, those who follow fashion believe they are freeing themselves from traditional morals, but they end up suffering under the dictatorship of fashion creators, who in turn have economic and ideological interests. A synchronised and uniform obedience, which follows the seasonal proclamation of

[5] *Ibid.*, p. 313.

an "official" fashion, reflects submission to the rules imposed by mass conformity. Fashion, which established itself in the nineteenth century, in the name of individuality, is able to spread itself only by imposing equal rules for everyone, and by reabsorbing the free manifestation of personal differences. According to the German sociologist George Simmel (1858–1918), fashion is the "obligatory modification of taste ... one of the many forms of life in which the tendencies to social equality and individual differentiation and variation come together to form a unit."[6]

2. THE FUNCTIONS OF CLOTHING

Fashion is expressed, above all, in how we dress. However, it is not only visible clothing, but the totality of invisible elements incorporated with it.[7] We must recall at this point that clothing tends to perform two different functions: the first is to help define our identity; the second is to protect the sense of modesty. The first function is practical, the second moral.

According to the *Encyclopedia Treccani*, "our clothing is a way of declaring to ourselves and to others who we are and what we do. Clothes have practical functions: they protect us from cold or heat, they are suited to the type of work we do. The mechanic wears overalls, the cook an apron, soldiers have uniforms. All peoples have a particular way of dressing, which can change over the centuries, but which allows a people to be identified ... Finally, in almost all cultures, clothing is also

---

[6] George Simmel, *La moda*, Editori Riuniti, Roma 1985, p. 51.
[7] Y. Kawamura, *La Moda*, cit., p. 11.

linked to a sense of modesty, a sentiment that is well rooted in man and not easy to explain. The sense of modesty varies in different historical periods, in different cultures, and from person to person."[8]

In a speech on 3 November 1957, Pius XII added to the practical and moral functions a third, aesthetic function, which he defines as "adornment": "Following that counsel of ancient wisdom, which considers the finality of things as the ultimate criterion both for any theoretical evaluation and for the certainty of moral principles, it will be useful to remember those aims that man has always established for himself when having recourse to clothing. Without doubt, he obeys the familiar requirements of hygiene, decency, and adornment. These are three necessities so deeply rooted in nature that they cannot be disregarded or contradicted without provoking repulsion and prejudice. They are as necessary today as they were yesterday; they are found among virtually every people; they can be seen at every level of the vast scale on which the natural necessity of clothing has been manifested, historically and ethnologically. It is important to note the strict interdependence which binds these three necessities, despite the fact that they derive from three different sources. The first is derived from man's physical nature; the second from his spiritual nature; the third from his psychological and artistic nature."[9]

[8.] Guido Fauro, article *Abbigliamento, Enciclopedia dei ragazzi*, Treccani, Roma 2005.
[9.] Pius XII, Address to the Participants of the First International Congress of Haute Couture, 8 November 1957.

With great wisdom, Pius XII praises fashion where it becomes an instrument of beauty, fulfilling its purpose of adornment. The young person seeks "attractive and splendid clothing which sing the happy themes of the springtime of life, and which facilitates, in harmony with the rules of modesty, the psychological prerequisites necessary for the formation of new families. At the same time, those of mature age seek appropriate clothing to enhance an aura of dignity, seriousness and serene happiness. In those cases where the aim is to enhance the moral beauty of the person, the style of clothes will be such as almost to eclipse physical beauty in the austere shadow of concealment, in order to distract the attention of the senses, and concentrate reflection on the spirit."[10]

The same pope, underlining the beauty of creation, encouraged master tailors to contemplate it, because "if plants and animals, then, are clothed in wonderful colours which attract the eye and admiration, cannot man imitate the Divine Artist in this?"[11] Clothing, then, has "its own multiform and efficacious language. At times, it is a spontaneous and faithful interpretation of sentiments and habits ... Clothing expresses joy and sorrow, authority and power, pride and simplicity, wealth and poverty, the sacred and the profane.[12]

---

[10] *Ibid.*

[11] Pius XII, Address to the International Congress of Master Tailors, 10 September 1954.

[12] Pius XII, Address to the Participants of the First International Congress of Haute Couture, cit.

Today, clothing no longer seems to reflect these criteria: the very function of protection from cold or heat is often sacrificed to the imperatives of fashion, which change the other principles, starting with the sense of shame. It suffices to consider what beaches are like today, as well as the spread of nudism, especially during the summer months, in large western cities.

The fashion revolution represents an attack on modesty, and must be seen in the context of a plan to reject beauty, which characterises the decadence of contemporary society. As Carmelo Leotta has noted "fashion only apparently becomes an instrument of beauty, if, in fact, beauty is never separated from the good and the true; the sensual ostentation of one's body becomes an instrument of disorder and renders love — naturally aimed at the perpetual possession of the true and the good — more difficult."[13]

3. FASHION AND CATHOLIC MORALITY

The primary aspect of the theme we are addressing is, of course, the moral aspect, which can be summarised in these words: fashions change throughout history, but Catholic morality does not change, because it is universal and absolute in its principles. The moral law is the criterion for judging fashion, which, by its nature, constantly changes.

---

[13] Carmelo Leotta, *«La via pulchritudinis»: La bellezza nella moda e nei costumi. La Quarta Rivoluzione* (http://www.scuoladieducazionecivile.org/la-bellezza-nella-moda-e-nei-costumi-la-quarta-rivoluzione/).

Fashion, therefore, must comply with the principles of morality, as Pius XII affirmed in a speech to the young women of Catholic Action on 22 May 1941: "What God asks of you is to always remember that fashion is not, nor can it be, the supreme rule of your conduct; that above fashion and its requirements, there are higher and more authoritative laws, superior and unchanging principles, which in no case can be sacrificed to the desire of pleasure or whim, and before which the idol of fashion must know how to bend its fleeting omnipotence. These are the principles that St Thomas Aquinas points to for feminine adornment, and recalls when he teaches us what the order of our charity and affections should be; the good of our soul has to come before that of our body, and to the advantage of our own body, we must prefer the good of the soul of our neighbour. Do you not see, then, that there is a limit that no style of fashion can overstep, beyond which, fashion becomes the mother of ruin for one's own soul and for others?"[14]

In a 1957 address to the Latin Union of Haute Couture, the same pontiff affirmed that, "the so-called relativity of fashions with respect to times, places, persons, and education is not a valid reason to renounce *a priori* a moral judgment on this or that fashion which, for the time being, violates the limits of normal decency. ... Yet, however broad and changeable the relative morals of styles may be, there is always an absolute norm to be kept, after having heard the admonitions of

---

[14.] Pius XII, Address to the Young Women of Catholic Action, 22 May 1941.

conscience, which warns against approaching danger: style must never be a proximate occasion of sin."

Pius XII expresses an absolute norm: if a fashion leads others to sin, it is intrinsically evil in itself and must be rejected by every Christian. This is an insurmountable moral limit. Fashion is immoral if it constitutes an occasion of sin for oneself or for others.

The expression "occasion of sin" refers to the possibility of sinning because of a person or thing. According to Catholic morality, the occasions of sin are divided into proximate (near) and remote. An occasion is called "proximate" when it causes serious danger, "remote" when it creates only a slight danger of sinning. "Proximate" is, therefore, the occasion that makes sin probable, even if it is not necessarily committed.[15]

Catholics have a grave obligation to flee occasions of sin. He who, without sufficient reason, does not flee the occasion of sin, by this very fact, commits a sin of the same kind that he places himself in danger of committing. This is why the popes have always warned against immoral fashions.

The judgments of Catholic morality on fashion are often dismissed as too rigid and overbearing, whilst every exaggeration and extravagance on the part of fashion is accepted without criticism.

[15.] Cardinals Pietro Palazzini and Francesco Roberti, *Dizionario di Teologia Morale*, Studium, Rome, 1961, p. 1006.

4. THE POPES AND FASHION

The popes of the twentieth century often intervened to remind the faithful not to be carried away by fashions which are immodest and unsuitable for a Catholic. Benedict XV (1914-1922), for example, deplored "the blindness of so many women, of every age and condition, who — made foolish by the desire to please — do not see to what degree they offend every honest man and offend God by the indecency of their clothing. Most of them would formerly have blushed at such ways of dressing as at a grave fault against Christian modesty. Now it does not suffice for them to exhibit them on the public thoroughfares; they do not even fear to cross the threshold of the churches, to assist at the holy sacrifice of the Mass, and even to bear the seductive food of shameful passions to the eucharistic table where one receives the heavenly Author of purity."[16]

Pius XI (1922–1939) spoke several times on the subject, both directly and through the Congregation of the Council, stating that: "Very often, when occasion arose, the same Supreme Pontiff emphatically condemned immodest fashion, adopted by Catholic women and girls, which not only offends the dignity of woman by defiling her adornment, but conduces to the temporal — and, still worse, to the eternal — ruin of women and girls, miserably dragging down others in their fall."[17] Addressing teaching sisters, Pius XI further stated: "Christian modesty of dress must be taught with insistence and 'at all costs'. And We

---

[16] Benedict XV, Encyclical *Sacra Propediem*, 6 January 1921.
[17] Letter of the Congregation of the Council, 12 January 1930.

wish the example to come from Catholic religious houses of education."[18]

Pius XII, in turn, admonished the young women of Catholic Action with these words: "It is not Our intention to trace out here the sad and all-too-well-known picture of the disorders which show themselves before your eyes, such as scanty clothes, (which seem to be made to reveal what they should instead veil) sports and exhibitions of 'camaraderie' in clothing that is irreconcilable with even the most permissive modesty; dances, shows, auditions, readings, illustrations, decorations in which the mania for fun and pleasure piles up the most serious dangers. Instead, We now intend to remind you and place again before your mind's eye the principles of the Christian faith which, in these matters, must enlighten your judgments, guide your steps and your conduct, and inspire and support your spiritual struggle."[19]

5. FASHION AND CHRISTIAN MORALS

The first criterion for judging fashion, especially as regards how to dress, is therefore moral. However, fashion is also the historical expression of a society's way of thinking and living and, in this respect, may also be subject to an historical (and not necessarily moral) judgment. In fact, the changes in fashion throughout history help us to understand the cultural and moral changes of a society, which in turn can be the subject-matter for a judgment of Christian philosophy or theology. Thus Pius

---

[18] Pius XI, Address to the International Union of Leagues of Catholic Women, 28 October 1925.
[19] Pius XII, Address to the Young Women of Catholic Action, cit.

XII affirmed that "society speaks through the clothing it wears; through its clothing, it reveals its secret aspirations and uses it, at least in part, to build or destroy its future."[20]

According to the teaching of the popes, the era that most perfectly expressed the Christian ideal of society was the Middle Ages, when "states were governed by the philosophy of the Gospel. Then, the power and divine virtue of Christian wisdom diffused itself throughout the laws, institutions, and morals of the people."[21] Medieval society and, as a whole, that also of the *Ancien Régime* prior to the French Revolution, were governed by principles based on tradition, ancient values and beliefs; these were not questioned, because they expressed the Christian identity: an identity defended over time and desired to be continued.

The decadence of the Christian Middle Ages, as Professor Plinio Corrêa de Oliveira observed, even before being an ideological decadence, was a decadence in morals with its origins in the disordered tendencies of man.[22]

One of the Brazilian thinker's key ideas was the importance he attributed to the role of tendencies and environments in the revolutionary process.[23] Environment is the harmony which results from the affinity of various beings gathered in the same place, and exerts a profound influence on men. All living

---

[20] Pius XII, Address to the Participants of the First International Congress of Haute Couture, cit.

[21] Leo XIII, Encyclical *Immortale Dei*, 1 November 1885.

[22] Plinio Corrêa de Oliveira, *Revolution and Counter-Revolution*, The American Society for the Defense of Tradition, Family and Property, Hanover, 2000.

[23] Roberto de Mattei, *Plinio Corrêa de Oliveira. Prophet of the Reign of Mary*, Preserving Christian Publications, Boonville, 2019.

beings, with man at the top, are part of the great environment of creation. Men in turn live in social environments, which exert a strong influence on tendencies and passions which become good or bad according to the purpose towards which they tend. Fashion is an expression of this social influence.

6. FASHION IN HUMANISM AND IN THE RENAISSANCE

The transition from the Middle Ages to the Renaissance, and humanism, can also be identified in the domain of fashion. According to historians, "the Middle Ages believed in difference, which made distinctions in dignity and functions, and applied them in theory and in practice; and clothes served to highlight and mark this .... Styles and colours of clothes communicated age, personal condition, social position and moods".[24] This vivacious spirit however was never spoiled by frivolity or sensuality. The change in cultural and moral tendencies began to take place in the fourteenth century.

The end of the Middle Ages was characterised by a revolution of morals, expressed, for example, by the shamelessness of Florentine women denounced by Dante.[25] The chronicler Giovanni Villani speaks of a "deformed change of dress" which took place in the first half of the fourteenth century, when long and wide dresses were replaced with a fashion of short and narrow dresses, and close-fitting doublets for men.[26] During the

---

[24] Maria Giuseppina Muzzarelli, *Guardaroba medievale. Vesti e società dal XIII al XVI secolo*, Il Mulino, Bologna, 1999, p. 15.

[25] Dante, *Purgatory*, Canto 23, 94-108.

[26] M. G. Muzzarelli, *Breve storia della moda in Itali*a, Il Mulino, Bologna 2011, p. 13.

humanist period, men's clothing accentuated the body, whilst women's fashion was characterised by curiosities.

Saint Antoninus of Florence (1389-1459) and Girolamo Savonarola (1452-1498) tried to put a stop to the immorality of fashion with the famous Bonfire of the Vanities.[27] So too did Saint Bernardine of Siena (1380-1444), with his Lenten sermons in 1420 and sermons preached on Piazza del Campo in 1427,[28] and Francesc Eiximenis (1330-1409) with his treatise *Llibre de les Dones*; all wanting to instruct the women of their time morally and practically.[29] Women's fashion of the fifteenth century, as St Bernardine described it, has many points in common with contemporary fashion: prevalent facial make up and long but revealing dresses. The saint especially drew attention to women in trousers, making it clear that this fashion is not suitable for woman's decency. He observed that it is forbidden by God, as we read in Deuteronomy 22:5: *Non induetur mulier veste virili* ("A woman shall not be clothed with man's apparel").[30]

---

[27] Cfr. also Odile Blanc, *Vêtement féminin, vêtement masculin à la fin du Moyen Age. Le point de vue des moralistes*, in O. Blanc, Pierre Bureau, Alice Planche, Perrine Mane, *Le vêtement. Histoire, archéologie et symbolique vestimentaires*, Le Léopard d'or, Paris, 1989, pp. 243-251.

[28] Saint Bernardine of Siena, *Lenten Sermons on the Christian Religion*, in *Opera omnia*, Quaracchi, Florence 1950, t. II: *Sermon XLIV, Contra mundanas vanitates et pompas*, pp. 45-58.

[29] Francesc Eiximenis, *Llibre de les dones, Critical edition* edited by Franck Naccarato, Curial, Barcelona 1981, 2 volumes.

[30] Diomede Scaramuzzi, *La frusta della moda*, in "Osservatore Romano", 17 July 1943.

The Catholic Counter-Reformation of the sixteenth and seventeenth centuries reacted on a doctrinal level, as well as on the level of customs. Plunging necklines disappeared and were replaced with high-necked dresses; and skirts were modelled in a stiff bell shape. The fashion from Italy was replaced by that of Spain. Black, a colour which is both elegant and austere, in contrast with white-collar workers, became the symbol of renunciation and asceticism.

7. FASHION DURING THE FRENCH REVOLUTION

In the era of the French Revolution, fashion rediscovered ancient pagan and Renaissance dress. Alexis de Tocqueville observed: "Never has fashion exercised a more extravagant and more fickle empire. A strange thing! Despair revived all the frivolity of ancient dress; only it had taken on a few new characteristics: it had become bizarre, disordered, and — so to speak — revolutionary: futile things, as well as serious things, lost their limit and their rule."[31]

Traditional Christian morality was based on the search for the good, the true and the beautiful, and had a high ideal of the purpose of life: the glory of God. These three concepts — the true, the good and the beautiful — are never separate: what is beautiful will also be true and good, and vice versa. When the desire for fashion takes over, there is a tendency to give importance to appearances, to the superfluous, and therefore to the love of oneself which replaces the love of God. Fashion

---

[31.] Alexis de Tocqueville, *Frammenti storici sulla Rivoluzione francese*, Ispi, Milan, 1943, p. 33.

for both men and women underwent a profound change during the French Revolution. The so-called "Phrygian cap", which was worn in ancient Rome by freed slaves, became the most popular headdress and went so far as to become a national dress, identical for everyone.

According to the historian Paul Johnson, "of all the permanent achievements of the French Revolution, the most important was the replacement of the *culottes* or breeches with the baggy trousers worn by the *sans-culottes* peasants and workers",[32] whence the term "sans-culottes" to refer to the revolutionaries. Some women, defined as "Amazons", even began to wear pantaloons.

Professor Plinio Corrêa de Oliveira observed: "The transformations that occurred over sixty years, from 1789 to 1848, led man to accept as good and normal something that was unnatural, cacophonous, grotesque, and Dantesque. And they gradually deformed men. Large industries, excessive speed, all these things deform man's subconscious... Little by little the world changed. From the standpoint of ambience and circumstance, the world changed far more between 1785 and 1885 than it did between 1885 and 1969. The world of 1785 had none of the inventions which emerged with the great steel industry — steam, electricity, and petroleum. In its material aspects, for example, this world [was] not much different from the world at the end of the Middle Ages. Conversely, in the

---

[32] Paul Johnson, *The Birth of the Modern*, 1815-1830, Tea, Milano 1991, pp. 431-432.

next one hundred years, everything changed. It was one of the greatest changes in history."[33]

To ensure that public opinion accepted these radical changes in the way of living, the Revolution especially made use of fashion. "Fashion was the great vehicle of the Revolution. In my opinion, it was an even more effective vehicle than the press; even more effective, I would add, than cinema and radio, which have been nothing but slaves to fashion. The resistance that the Industrial Revolution might have encountered was shattered by fashion. Fashion has instilled the idea that man (the true man, the authentically virile man) should adapt to noise, to bad smells, to excessive speed, to every thrill that progress imposes on nature; and adapt himself to it — not in a resigned way, but euphorically — finding that it is good, that it is the ideal. Anyone who did not accept this new environment with due zeal was considered a fool, an idiot, an ignoramus."[34]

8. THE END OF THE *BELLE ÉPOQUE*

At the turn of the twentieth century, the so-called *Belle Époque*, with its sweetness of life, still expressed a way of dressing and behaving inspired by Catholic tradition and morality. During the 1800s, fashion was mainly dictated by France. The figure of the *couturier*, the tailor-artist who interprets the "signs of the times" had established itself with Jean-Philippe Worth (1825–1895). Sketches of the models he created spread from Paris to Vienna, London, and St Petersburg. With him, fashion

---

[33] Cit. in R. de Mattei, *The Prophet of the Reign of Mary*, cit., pp. 217-218.
[34] *Ibid.*, p. 218.

became a creative enterprise, an advertising show and, above all, an international sensation.[35]

Until the *Belle Époque*, the parts of the woman's body which were visible had been very limited: her hands, her face and nothing else. Women continued to go out wearing hats, according to the Pauline dictate (1 Cor 11) which required, as a sign of humility, that they not appear in public with their heads uncovered. The dress was closed at the neck, the body concealed by long skirts. "It was the face above all that had to communicate grace and care."[36] The woman maintained her role as mother and guardian of the family order, and the bearer of values and virtue.

The First World War caused a cultural and social upheaval that was expressed in the dizzying libertarian and egalitarian acceleration of fashion. "At the end of the 1910s, and especially during the 1920s," writes Carlo Arturo Quintavalle, "the Soviet progressives and constructivist movement rethought the social function of dress and suggested non-customary models; indeed they were profoundly indecent. The sources of this revolution were to be found in cubist culture, in the recovery of primitive arts and popular traditions, in the futurist movement, which was the subject of lively discussion in Moscow, and also thanks to the influence of Filippo Tommaso Marinetti. All these causes, however, were integrated and transformed into the revolutionary perspective of the confrontation between classes, in which the rejection of bourgeois dress and traditional fashion was

---

[35] Sofia Gnoli, *Un secolo di moda italiana 1900-2000*, Meltemi, Rome, 2005.
[36] M. G. Muzzarelli, *Breve storia della moda in Italia*, cit., p. 140.

identified with new behaviours, purposes and experiences. The critique which informs these models obviously rejects the 'culture of traditional dress' and fashion, understood in their historical sense, and accepts only the creation of subversive and, therefore, symbolically revolutionary clothes."[37]

The war took away many men, and women were pushed to take their place both in the country and in cities: women thus entered factories, public offices, schools. "The image of the woman at home and with her family," observes Gioia Cesarini, "slowly began to fade, and the signs of this revolution are evident in post-war women's clothing."[38]

On the international level, the forerunner of this new style was the French designer Coco Chanel (pseudonym of Gabrielle Bonheur, 1883–1971), whose fashion house revolutionised the concept of femininity, promoting the *garçonne style*,[39] a masculine look for women: business suits, skirts shortened to knee height, and the novelty of very short hair, combined with a very thin body, thus ushering in the era of slimming diets.[40] Chanel's fashion revolution coincided with the explosion of the feminist

---

[37] Carlo Arturo Quintavalle, article *Moda*, in *Enciclopedia Italiana di Scienze, Lettere, Arti*, Istituto della Enciclopedia Italiana founded by Giovanni Treccani, App. V, 1993, Vol. III, p. 509.

[38] Gioia Cesarini, *La moda attraverso i secoli*, Editrice Italiana Roma, Rome, 1964, p. 145.

[39] The [French] feminine term "garçonne" derives from the masculine "garçon". It became popular with the success of Victor Margheritte's novel *La Garçonne* (1922), which caused wide debate over the new concept of femininity described by the author.

[40] Cfr. *Moda, in Lessico Universale Italiano*, vol. 14, Istituto della Enciclopedia Italiana, Rome, 1974, p. 56.

movement.[41] It was she who introduced the use of women's trousers — not popular, however, in the 1930s.

Between the World Wars, Hollywood's motion picture industry also influenced our way of life. Women tried to look like the most famous actresses by copying their haircut or clothes. Other factors played a major role in the women's revolution. Women's sportswear contributed to their emancipation; their engagement in sports, such as skiing, tennis, and cycling allowed them to change clothing styles, and to initiate a process of undressing the female body. Alongside sports, the notion of comfort also influenced ways of dressing, becoming synonymous with a psycho-physical state of wellbeing.

"This first revolutionary attack," Plinio Corrêa de Oliveira observes, "was shortly to be followed by a reaction imposed by common sense and modesty. Skirts and sleeves lengthened again. Through successive variations, women's fashion reached limits very close to those of what, in today's language, could be called the 'early years' of 1916–1917, before the revolution in clothing recovered the lost ground through new daring. This boldness was usually followed by reactions — and again by new daring — and in such a way that its audacity was always greater than the reaction."[42]

---

[41] Martina Bitunjac, *La donna non si metterà un indumento da uomo… La differenza di genere e la storia en travesti*, in *La moda contiene la storia e ce la racconta puntualmente*, edited by Giovanna Motta, Edizioni Nuova Cultura, Rome, 2015, pp. 229-238.

[42] Plinio Corrêa de Oliveira, *Dove va la rivoluzione nell'abbigliamento?*, in "Cristianità", no. 5 (1974), p. 12.

9. FASHION AFTER WORLD WAR II

According to Lipovetsky, the eruption of *prêt-à-porter* ("ready-to-wear") clothes in the 1950s destroyed the fashion structure of the previous hundred years.[43] The success of department stores, which became more and more widespread from the second half of the nineteenth century, is linked to the democratic revolution of *prêt-à-porter*: Les Passages, Bon Marché, Samaritaine and La Fayette in France, Harrods and Selfridges in Great Britain, Brooks Brothers in the United States. The department store would develop in Italy at the beginning of the twentieth century with Rinascente, Upim and Standa. Department stores throughout the world contributed to the success of mass consumption and favoured "the propagation of fashion even among the lower and middle classes".[44]

The fashion house of Christian Dior (1905–1957), established in 1946, reacted against the Chanel style with a new look which returned to the long skirts of the *Belle Époque*; in the sixties, however, the miniskirt was launched — in France by André Courreges (1923–2016) and in England by Mary Quant. Miniskirts, jeans, long hair, and beat music were an expression of the libertarian revolution of '68.

"I love vulgarity. Good taste is death, vulgarity is life."[45] According to Luis Sergio Solimeo, "these words of the English fashion designer Mary Quant, who took credit for inventing

---

[43] G. Lipovetsky, *L'empire de l'éphémère*, cit., p. 128.

[44] Cinzia Capalbo, *L'evoluzione del retail in età contemporanea*, in *La moda contiene la storia*, cit., p. 255 (pp. 239-257).

[45] *Mary Quant talks to Alison Adburgham, in The Guardian*, 10 October 1967 (https://www.theguardian.com/century/1960-1969/Story/0,,106475,00.html).

miniskirts and hot pants, reveal one of the most important, though rarely observed, aspects of the 'fashion revolution' which started in the sixties: vulgarity. Indeed, fashions have tended increasingly toward vulgarity. Vulgarity not only tramples on good taste and decorum but reflects a mentality opposed to all order and discipline, and to every kind of restraint — be it aesthetic, moral or social — and which ultimately suggests a completely 'liberated' standard of behaviour."[46]

The liberalisation of morals, which the new fashion expresses, also involves a strong tendency towards egalitarianism. "There is a general tendency in our times to establish a most radical egalitarianism at all levels of culture, in social relations between the sexes, and even between men and animals. In dress, this egalitarianism is manifested by a growing proletarianisation, by the establishment of unisex fashions and by the abolition of differences between generations. The same garb can be worn by anybody no matter his position, age or circumstance (e.g. on a trip, or at a religious or civil ceremony). Chaos reigns today in the domains of fashion. It is often difficult to distinguish — by their clothes — men from women, parents from children, a religious ceremony from a picnic. Haircuts and hairstyles follow the same tendency, confounding age and sex, and breaking down standards of elegance and good taste."[47]

Also in the 1960s, blue jeans spread — patented by the German-born (but naturalised American) entrepreneur, Levi

---

[46] Luis Sergio Solimeo, *Modesty and God*, https://tfpstudentaction.org/blog/modesty-and-god.
[47] *Ibid.*

Strauss (1829–1902). In 1962, Wrangler opened its first factory in Belgium, where another American jeans company, Lee, also set up a shop in 1964. The garment used since the mid-nineteenth century by workers in factories became a symbol of the new egalitarian revolution.

10. THE REVOLUTION AND FASHION OF '68

1968 marked a radical turning point in western social life, and the change it produced in clothing and behaviour, especially for women, was no less marked.

But the clothing revolution of 1968 had already been prepared by the major designers of the era. Claude Brouet (editor-in-chief of *Elle* magazine from 1953 to 1969) wrote: "I don't have much to say about the style of 1968, for the good reason that everything was already there! Miniskirts, sheer tights, nylon stockings, jeans. 'Young fashion', as it was called, was born in 1965 and 1966 with the emergence of designers."[48]

The fashion historian Xavier Chaumette also confirms the importance of this moment for the industry: "There had already been some phases of emancipation in the 1920s but, at the end of the 1960s, times were good because they had succeeded! Youth came to power and clothing fully expressed this. Women were emancipated and wore miniskirts and trousers. We wanted garments with fewer social connotations. The wind blowing from the left invited us to move away from work uniforms: Mao jackets, cowboy jeans, mechanic t-shirts,

[48] https://madame.lefigaro.fr/style/la-mode-na-pas-attendu-mai-68-pour-faire-sa-revolution-080218-146857.

farmer corduroys ... And then, of course, there was the fantastic rise of ready-made clothing that allowed everyone to dress fashionably."[49]

Already, in 1966, the fashion house of Yves Saint-Laurent (1936-2008), a true radar of trends, presented its *prêt-à-porter* collection in Paris, introducing women's trousers as a new symbol of elegance. The dictates of fashion houses were to simplify clothes and overturn the traditional criteria of how to dress. "1966," argues Xavier Chaumette, "marked the end of the dictates of clothing. In big cities, emancipated women enjoyed being provocative and didn't care if they were called vulgar or aggressive. They had short or loose hair, and ultra-short skirts and trousers, even if they were still banned in many institutions."[50] The bourgeois dress of mothers, in Chanel and Balenciaga, bored the daughters. The same historian continues: "The stylistic evolution, which started a century earlier, seemed very slow. The sixties would be like a bomb, allowing freedom and movement; the new clothing broke all chains."[51]

The egalitarian demands of 1968 were thus manifested in clothing, imposing a uniform on everyone in order to eliminate social differences. The criteria of beauty, decorum, harmony, elegance, which were already in crisis, were overcome by the egalitarian and anarchic spirit that was the very soul of the

---

[49.] https://www.elle.fr/Mode/Les-news-mode/Mode-que-reste-t-il-de-mai-68-3685007.
[50.] https://madame.lefigaro.fr/style/la-mode-na-pas-attendu-mai-68-pour-faire-sa-revolution-080218-146857.
[51.] *Ibid.*

movement. In 1968, most of the girls at demonstrations were in trousers. Jeans became a sort of uniform for the youth, the quintessential symbol of the new egalitarian fashion. "There was nothing more rebellious than jeans!" Chaumette concluded. "The 'look of the left' was renewed in May of '68: overalls, sweaters, jackets with Korean collars, clothes purchased at military surplus stores. Before the barricades, intellectuals and young people had already dreamed of popular uniforms, but it was at this moment that they fully made these their own."[52]

However, this did not only happen in France. "The connection between hairstyles and the political climate is now so close that, among the extreme Italian left, clothing styles, messy hair and unkempt beards have even taken the place of thought, logic, and ideology."[53] Controversy itself was a fashion. "It was the collective and subjective present that was the focal point of May '68, the first fashion revolution, where the frivolous prevailed over the tragic, where the historical merged with the playful."[54]

Haute couture also underwent a revolution. In 1968, Yves Saint-Laurent proclaimed, *"A bas le Ritz, vive la rue"* ("Down with the Ritz, long live the street"). The beginning of the 1970s also saw a tendency towards nudism, which on beaches had been nearly accomplished already with "bikini" bathing suits, manifesting controversial social "taboos".

---

[52] *Ibid.*
[53] Luigi Barzini, *Dimmi come ti vesti*, in *Il Giornale*, 1 April 1978.
[54] G. Lipovetsky, *L'empire de l'éphémère*, cit., p. 289.

11. THE FASHION REVOLUTION PREPARING FOR GENDER THEORY

Aggressive and flashy punk fashion first appeared in London in the 1970s. "It was an anarchistic and nihilistic style, which deliberately aimed to traumatise society."[55] Shaved heads, dirty and torn clothes, black clothes with metal studs constituted a challenge not only to traditional clothing, but to the values of western culture. If punk fashion marked the eruption of chaos in the way of everyday dress, an even stronger attack on the cultural and moral order was launched by unisex fashion, which challenged male and female identities through the "neutralisation" of clothing. The criterion of unisex fashion is egalitarianism between the sexes.

When, in the 1950s, Claude Lévy-Strauss (1908–2009) and Michel Foucault (1926–1984) began to differentiate "sex" from "gender", they did nothing but take up theories, advanced by scholars almost a century earlier, which anticipated a social anthropology of dress and gender. The still academic-sounding theories of Lévy-Strauss and Foucault were realised in the birth of unisex clothing. "Clothes no longer reflect one's identity. In other words, they no longer indicate a person's social position, profession or even more fundamental characteristics, such as a person's sex and age ... Thus, unisex clothing has become very popular: jeans and shorts are worn by people of both sexes and of all generations. Young men and women, the young and the old, single and married people, teachers and students,

---

[55] Y. Kawamura, *La moda*, cit., p. 138.

children and adults, all mix and wear the same dress that no longer expresses what they are, think or want."[56]

A decisive role was played by the Austrian designer Rudi Gernreich (1922–1985), a homosexual activist who, with his "partner" Harry Hay (1912–2002), founded the Mattachine Society in 1954, the first organisation promoting homosexual liberation in the United States."

Gernreich exerted a profound influence on fashion, anticipating the "fluidity between genders". He invented the first topless bathing suit and experimented, in his Unisex Project, with dressing male and female models with identical clothes.

Along these lines, gender studies, which developed within American feminism in the 1970s, placed at the centre of their conceptual approach the denial of an authentic difference between man and woman. "Gender" — male or female — is no longer a biological and real fact, but a fluid social construction, a fluctuating and subjective identity.[57] The woman must finally feel "freed" from the stereotype instilled by patriarchal society; she must be able to do everything a man does: to work like a man, to dress like a man. Trousers make her feel like a man. Her way of being suffers; from being maternal, sensitive, and sweet, she often becomes selfish, tough, and aggressive.

Through the unisex style, women become masculine, whilst men tend towards femininity: giving excessive attention to clothing, fine fabrics and garments; the typical colours of women — pink, red, purple — become favourable colours

---

[56.] https://tfpstudentaction.org/blog/modesty-and-god.
[57.] Rodolfo de Mattei, *Gender Diktat*, Solfanelli, Chieti 2014, pp. 44-45.

for men's clothes displayed at fashion shows. In Italy, Giorgio Armani began his career with the inversion of male and female standards: feminising men and masculinising women.

All this influences the mentality of the man on the street, who now accepts these interchangeable roles between the male and female "genders". In 2013 Gender Fusion was launched — the "neutral" fashion intended for those who do not recognise themselves in the old stereotypes of male and female.[58] The concept which is being passed on is that the male-female difference is merely a cultural and not a natural fact. And, since culture can change, the next step is to suggest the interchangeability in practice — through medical means which offer surgical operations to make a man "a woman" and a woman "a man". And, precisely in order to make this utopia a normality, it must be imposed in schools, indoctrinating children from an early age. Clothing is once again a revolutionary tool: in kindergartens and schools where gender ideology is applied, boys dress as girls and girls as boys; boys can have their nails painted and they are being taught embroidery or crocheting, whilst girls devote themselves to disassembling engines or playing with toy cars.

12. THE NECESSARY REACTION

Fashion is therefore a formidable revolutionary weapon and needs to be contested when it threatens to invert not only the principles of Catholic morality, but the very core values of western culture. Already in 1919, Pope Benedict XV called

[58] *Ibid.*, p. 116.

upon the Catholic Women's Union to form a league in order to fight indecent fashions, emphasising that "Christian courage — which gives life to the good example of woman, both in the polluted environment of our age and in the face of the spread of indecent fashions — also facilitates the whole mission of woman in society, so that the same vernacular language expresses a dictate of common sense when it says that virtue is obligatory."[59]

In 1928, a real "crusade" against immodest fashions was declared by Pius XI who, through the Sacred Congregation for Religious, warned all schools, academies, recreational centres and workshops directed by religious sisters that "those girls who do not observe the rules of Christian modesty and decency in dress should not be admitted".[60] The same recommendations were given by the Congregation of the Council on 12 January 1930 and Pope Pius XI himself exhorted young Catholics not to hesitate but to "resolutely continue to fight the good fight in which it is a question of the honour of God and His Church and, at the same time, of their honour, dignity, and all that they have which is most beautiful, most glorious, most precious".[61]

In those years, the magazine of the Catholic Women's Movement, *Squilli di Risurrezione* ("Rings of Resurrection"), invited its members always to dress in the most proper way, according to their social status. The two extremes to avoid were

---

[59] Benedict XV, Address to the Directors of the Italian Catholic Women's Union, 22 October 1919.

[60] Letter of the Congregation for Religious, 23 August 1928.

[61] Pius XI, Address to the Female Catholic Youth of Rome, 20 June 1926.

considered "the epidemic of luxury" and the "democratisation of clothing". In fact, sloppiness was considered the daughter of a false piety and a distorted vision of Christian life, according to which we should renounce that beauty and elegance which can serve as instruments of the apostolate and the foundation of an authentically Christian fashion.[62]

On 6 October 1940, a few months after his election, Pius XII addressed the young women of Catholic Action, stating that: "Fashion and modesty should walk together like two sisters, because both words have the same etymology, from the Latin *modus* — that is, the right measure, beyond which one cannot find the right way. But modesty is no longer in fashion. Similar to those poor alienated people who, having lost the instinct for self-preservation, along with the notion of danger, throw themselves either into the fire or into the river; not a few female souls, made oblivious to Christian modesty by ambitious vanity, woefully face dangers in which their purity may find death. They give in to the tyranny of fashion, even when it is immodest, and in such a way as not even to suspect that it is unbecoming. They have lost the very concept of danger: they have lost the instinct of modesty."[63]

And, on 22 May 1941, while World War II was raging, Pius XII stressed the need for a "crusade" against those who threaten Christian morality,[64] pointing to the responsibility

---

[62] Anna Praitoni, *Fate la guerra alle mode indecenti. La donna cattolica tra apostolato e modernizzazione (1919-1928)*, in *Dimensioni e Problemi della Ricerca storica*, Booklet 1 (1995), pp. 259-268.

[63] Pius XII, Address to the Young Women of Catholic Action, 6 October 1940.

[64] Pius XII, Address, 22 May 1951.

of the press, the cinema and variety shows. According to the same pope, it is very important to recognise that fashion has an influence on society and, through it, on the common man, for better or for worse. "But the Christian," he would later reiterate, "whether he be creator or client, should be careful not to underestimate the dangers and spiritual ruin spread by immodest fashions, because of that continuity which must exist between what one preaches and what one practices."[65]

Other popes after Pius XII do not appear to have addressed the question of fashion and its consequences, firstly for women, but cascading over the whole of society. Indeed, beginning with the Second Vatican Council (1962–1965), it would seem that the women's revolution, or rather the feminist revolt, has accelerated within the Church herself, leading to a profound change in the clothing and behaviour of priests, and of male and female religious.

Faced with such decadence of morals, women are especially called to react, and must begin by becoming aware of the meaning of the phenomenon of fashion. "Women and young Catholics," Pius XII exhorts, "you would have thought once upon a time of faithfully fulfilling your mission, a sacred and fruitful mission in the care of a healthy, strong and serene family; or you would have thought of devoting your life to the service of God, recollected in the cloister or in the works of an apostolate and charity. Beautiful ideals in which woman finds

---

[65] Pius XII, Address to the Participants of the First International Congress of Haute Couture, cit.

her true place and can exercise a beneficial action around her without making a fuss! Instead, you now appear in public, you go into the arena to take part in the fight. You have neither sought nor provoked it; you accept it valiantly; not as resigned victims in a courageous but purely defensive resistance — you go instead on the counterattack and for the conquest."[66]

The following texts constitute the doctrinal foundations of a moral revival which, starting from fashion, could extend to the whole of society. In fact, through our clothing we express a world vision — and, if it is true that examples count as much as ideas, it is also in the way we dress that we will be able to express our "lived Christianity".

---

[66] Pius XII, Address to the Delegates of the International Female Catholic Union, 11 September 1947.

The Teaching of the Popes from Benedict XV to Pius XII (1914–1958)

BENEDICT XV (1914–1922)

I Address to the Directors of the Italian Catholic Women's Union, 22 October 1919

The changed conditions of the times have conferred on woman roles and rights that the previous age did not grant her. But no change in the action of men, nor any novelty in things and events, can ever distance the woman who is aware of her mission from her natural centre, which is her family. She is queen in the domestic hearth; and even when she is far from home, she must direct there, not only the affection of a mother, but also the care of a wise ruler — in the same way that a sovereign, who is outside the territory of his own State, does not neglect its good but always keeps it at the top of his thoughts.

Therefore, it can be rightly said that the changed conditions of the times have enlarged the field of female activity: an apostolate for women, in the midst of the world has followed that more intimate and restricted action which she previously carried out at home; but even today, this apostolate must be accomplished in such a way as to make it clear that women, both outside and inside the home, must not forget the duty to devote themselves mainly to their family.

It is with no other criterion that we now intend to form the growing — and ever more increasing — activity of Italian Catholic women. We therefore applaud the firm intention of "dedication to the education of the youth, and to the improvement of the family and of the school". We do not overlook the rights claimed by those wishing to freely educate children, because it would be barbaric to pretend that those who are no strangers to the formation of the humblest part of children should be kept away from the care and development of their noblest part.

Let us hasten instead to rejoice at the resolution that has been made to ensure that the Catholic woman has a sense of her duty, not only to be upstanding, but to show herself as such in the way she dresses. Such a purpose expresses the need for the good example that the Catholic woman must give. And oh! How serious, how urgent is the duty to repudiate those exaggerations of fashion, which are the result of corruption in their inventors and, as the most worthy President of the Catholic Women's Union has just warned, bring a nefarious contribution to the general corruption of customs.

Current excesses

We believe that We must insist on this point particularly because, on the one hand, We know that certain styles of dress which have come into use among women today are harmful to the good of society; and on the other hand, it fills Us with amazement and astonishment to see that those who supply the poison seem unaware of its evil effect, and whoever sets fire to the house seems unaware of its destructive force. The mere supposition of such ignorance makes fathomable the deplorable spread of what has taken place in our day: a fashion so contrary to that modesty which should be the most beautiful adornment of the Christian woman. Without such ignorance, it seems to Us that no woman could have gone so far as to use indecent garments even in approaching the sacred place — in presenting herself, even, to the natural and most accredited masters of Christian morality.

The duty to react

Oh! With what satisfaction therefore have we understood that the members of the Catholic Women's Union have written in their programme the intention of presenting themselves decently even in the style of dressing. By doing so, they will fulfil the strict duty of not giving scandal — of not being a stumbling block on the path of virtue — and they will also show that, having expanded their mission in the world, they understand the need to set a good example, no longer only among those at home, but also in the streets and even public squares.

The necessity of this is such that, in recognising it, Catholic women must feel constrained, not only by individual obligation, but also by social duty. We therefore would like the numerous members of the Catholic Women's Union gathered today in Our presence to form a league among themselves in order to combat indecent fashions, not only in themselves, but also in all those persons or families whom they may effectively reach by their work. It is unnecessary to add that a good mother must never allow her daughters to yield to the false demands of a fashion which is not perfectly disciplined; but it bears saying that, the higher the position a lady occupies, the stricter her duty not to suffer anyone who visits her to dare offend her modesty by dressing indecently. A warning given in time would prevent the repetition of such bold impertinence and the violation of the well-established rights of hospitality. And a timely echo of reproach may even dissuade other unwary advocates of unseemly fashions not to stain themselves with those fashions which are disgraceful, as it would any wise lady.

We believe that fathers, husbands, brothers and all relatives of these brave warrioresses should make the best of this league against vice; we would like sacred pastors, and indeed all priests responsible for the care of souls, to promote and present it in the best possible way, in all places where fashion has crossed the boundaries of modesty ... and it has unfortunately crossed them in many places! But may Our word be received chiefly by you, Our most beloved daughters, who have declared today that you want to engage in an apostolate in the midst of the world.

One must not believe, however, that good example benefits only the educational work that belongs to women directly, both in and outside the family. Indeed, Christian courage — which gives life to the good example of woman, both in the polluted environment of our age and in the face of the spread of indecent fashions — also facilitates the whole mission of woman in society, so that the same vernacular language expresses a dictate of common sense when it says that virtue is obligatory.

The programme of action

But let Us go back, dearest daughters, to the examination of your intentions (which We mean to commend). We have understood with pleasure that the Catholic Women's Union "promises in particular to dedicate itself to the education of youth and to the improvement of the family and of the school".

It is in this, principally, that We are happy to have been pre-empted in Our desires, for if We had to give a programme of women's action, We could draw up no better rules than those which aim at the good of the youth, of the family and of schools. And not only do We praise the end, but We applaud the means to be used: "bringing, as has been clearly stated, a clearer vision of justice and charity to the whole life of the country". Oh! If new generations grew up instructed in these virtues — and above all, if justice and charity were discussed less and practised more — they would soon find excellent solutions to much-debated social questions.

To achieve such a desirable effect, Catholic women should also insist on the duty of parents to demand religious education for their children; you should insist on the obligation of civil authorities not to hinder you, and above all, you should insist on the need to ask the Church for the most appropriate rules of action, in order to put them into practice.

But since the need for the apostolate of women is great, since the urgency to stop evil and to make good flourish outstrips every effort possible to creatures, We raise our gaze to Heaven; from Heaven alone can come the most powerful help, and to Heaven We confidently address Our prayer.

Thus, as it could be said of a single misled individual that he was led back to a good path by the fidelity of a woman; *santificatus est vir infidelis per mulierem fidelem* — "the unbelieving husband is sanctified by the believing wife" (1 Cor 7:14); so may it soon be repeated of today's society, returned to the life of salvation through examples and teachings — in a word, through the mission of Catholic woman.

II *Sacra Propediem*, Encyclical on the Third Order of St Francis, 6 January 1921

There are two dominant passions today in the profound lawlessness of morals: an unlimited desire for riches and an insatiable thirst for pleasures. Our epoch is marked with a shameful stigma: whilst it goes ceaselessly from progress to progress in the order of wellbeing and convenience of life, it seems that, in the superior order of decency and moral rectitude, a lamentable worsening leads it back to the ignominies of ancient paganism.

Truthfully, in the measure that men lose sight of the eternal goods that Heaven has reserved for them, they permit themselves to be more taken in by the deceitful mirage of ephemeral goods here below, and once their souls are turned down towards the earth, an easy descent leads them insensibly to become lax in virtue, to experience repugnance for spiritual things, and to relish nothing outside the seductions of pleasure. Hence the general situation which we note: for some, the desire to acquire riches knows no bound, whilst others no longer know how to bear — as formerly — the trials which are the usual result of want or poverty; and, at the very hour in which the rivalries that We have pointed out pit the proletariat against the rich, a great many people seem anxious to provoke further hatred from the poor by an unbridled luxury which accompanies the most revolting corruption.

From this point of view, one cannot sufficiently deplore the blindness of so many women, of every age and condition, who — made foolish by the desire to please — do not see to what degree they offend every honest man and offend God by the indecency of their clothing. Most of them would formerly have blushed at such ways of dressing as at a grave fault against Christian modesty. Now it does not suffice for them to exhibit them on the public thoroughfares; they do not even fear to cross the threshold of the churches, to assist at the holy sacrifice of the Mass, and even to bear the seductive food of shameful passions to the eucharistic table where one receives the heavenly Author of purity. And We say nothing of those exotic and barbarous dances, recently imported into fashionable circles, each more shocking than the last. One cannot imagine anything more suitable for banishing all the remains of modesty.

In considering attentively this state of things, tertiaries will understand what our epoch expects from the disciples of St Francis, whom they call the *Poverello* ("little pauper") and who received in his flesh the stigmata of the Crucified One. If they bring their attention back to the life of their father, they will see what perfect and living resemblance he had to Jesus Christ — above all, in His flight from satisfactions and his love of the trials of this life. It is for them to show that they remain worthy of him by embracing poverty, at least in spirit, by renouncing themselves, and by each one bearing his cross.

In that which especially concerns tertiary sisters, We ask of them, by their dress and manner of wearing it, to be models of holy modesty for other ladies and for young girls, so that they may be thoroughly convinced that the best way for them to be of use to the Church and to society is to labour for the improvement of morals.

PIUS XI (1922-1939)

I Letter of the Congregation for Religious, 23 August 1928

To the ordinaries of Italy: as regards the crusade against immodest fashions, especially in schools run by teaching sisters.

Circular letter against immodest fashion
Most illustrious and reverend lords, you are well aware of the grave words of condemnation that the Holy Father has pronounced, with his apostolic authority, on several occasions against immodest fashions in female dress, which prevail today to the detriment of good comportment. It is enough to recall the very grave words, full of pain and warning, with which His Holiness — in the speech of last 15 August, in the Consistorial Chamber, promulgating the decree on the heroic virtues of Venerable Paola Frassinetti — once again denounced the danger, which threatens with its seductive charm so many unwary souls who profess to belong to the flock of Jesus Christ and of His Holy Church.

It is painful to underline, in this regard, that deplorable fashion tends to creep in — even among young girls who attend some of the schools run by teaching sisters, and into Sunday school classes held in women's religious institutions.

To face the danger, which is becoming more serious the further it spreads, this Sacred Congregation, by order of the Holy Father, draws to the attention of the ordinaries of Italy the following injunctions, confirmed by His Holiness in today's audience, so that they may communicate them to the superiors of religious houses in their respective dioceses:

1. From now on, in all schools, academies, recreational centres, Sunday schools and workshops run by religious sisters, those girls who do not observe the rules of Christian modesty and decency in dress should not be admitted.

2. To this end, the superiors themselves will be obliged to exercise strict supervision, and to peremptorily exclude from their institutions' schools and projects those pupils who do not comply with these prescriptions.

3. They must not be influenced in this by any human respect, nor by material considerations, nor by reasons of their pupils' social and family prestige, even if the student body were to decrease as a result.

4. In addition to carrying out their educational activities, the sisters must strive to instil in their pupils, gently but firmly, the love and taste for holy modesty, a sign and guard of the purity and delicate adornment of women.

Your supervision will be vigilant, that these injunctions may be observed exactly, and that there may be a perfect conformity of conduct among all the religious institutes of the diocese. You will reprimand severely anyone who is disobedient in this and notify this Sacred Congregation if any abuse is perpetrated.

With the highest esteem,

Camillo Cardinal Laurenti,
Prefect of the Sacred Congregation for Religious
Vincent Lapuma,
Secretary

II Letter of the Congregation of the Council, 12 January 1930

Against indecent fashion

By virtue of the supreme apostolate which he wields over the Universal Church by divine will, our Most Holy Father Pope Pius XI has never ceased to inculcate, verbally and by his writings, the exhortation of St Paul to women: "adorning themselves with modesty and sobriety ... professing godliness with good works" (1 Tim 2:9–10).

Very often, when occasion arose, the same Supreme Pontiff emphatically condemned immodest fashion, adopted by Catholic women and girls, which not only offends the dignity of woman by defiling her adornment, but conduces to the temporal — and, still worse, to the eternal — ruin of women and girls miserably dragging down others in their fall. It is not surprising, therefore, that all bishops and other ordinaries, as is the duty of ministers of Christ, should have unanimously opposed depraved licentiousness and promiscuity of manners in their own dioceses, often bearing with fortitude the derision and mockery levelled against them for this cause.

Therefore this Sacred Council, which watches over the discipline of the clergy and the people, while cordially commending the action of these venerable bishops, most emphatically exhorts them to persevere in their attitude and increase their activities insofar as their strength permits, in order that this unwholesome disease may be definitively uprooted from human society.

In order to facilitate the desired effect, this Sacred Congregation, by the mandate of the Most Holy Father, has decreed as follows:

Exhortation to those in authority

1. Parish priests, and preachers especially, when occasion arises, should "reprove, entreat, rebuke", according to the words of the Apostle Paul (2 Tim 4:2), that feminine garb, based on modesty and womanly adornment, may be a defence of virtue. Let them likewise admonish parents to ensure that their daughters cease to wear indecorous dress.

2. Parents, conscious of their grave obligations in the education (especially religious and moral) of their children,

should see to it that their daughters are solidly instructed, from earliest childhood, in Christian doctrine; that they themselves assiduously inculcate in their souls, by word and example, love for the virtues of modesty and chastity; and since their family should follow the example of the Holy Family, they must rule in such a way that all its members, raised within the walls of the home, should find reason and incentive to love and preserve modesty.

3. Let parents keep their daughters away from public gymnastic games and contests; but if their daughters are compelled to attend such exhibitions, let them see that they are fully and modestly dressed. Let them never permit their daughters to don immodest garb.

4. Superiors and teachers in schools for girls must do their utmost to instil love of modesty in the hearts of the maidens confided to their care, and urge them to dress modestly.

5. The same superiors and teachers must not receive in their colleges and schools immodestly dressed girls, nor make an exception for the mothers of pupils. If such pupils, after being admitted, persist in dressing immodestly, they should be expelled.

6. Nuns, in compliance with the letter of the Sacred Congregation of Religious, dated 23 August 1928, must not

admit into their colleges, schools, oratories or recreation grounds — nor tolerate, if already admitted — girls who do not dress with Christian modesty; the same sisters, in addition, should do their utmost that the love of holy chastity and Christian modesty may become deeply rooted in the hearts of their pupils.

7. It is desirable that pious organisations of women be founded which, by their counsel, example and publicity should combat the wearing of apparel unsuited to Christian modesty, and should promote purity of customs and modesty of dress.

8. Those who dress immodestly should not be admitted into these pious associations of women; and if, perchance, having been admitted, they fall again into their error, they should be dismissed forthwith.

9. Maidens and women who dress immodestly are to be debarred from Holy Communion and from acting as sponsors in the sacraments of Baptism and Confirmation; further, if the offence be extreme, they may even be forbidden to enter the church.

Donato Cardinal Sbaretti,
Prefect of the Congregation of the Council

PIUS XII (1939–1958)

I Address to the Young Women of Catholic Action, 6 October 1940

Fashion and modesty

Therefore, you who so piously dress the altar and the dwelling of Jesus Christ: never forget that you yourselves carry God within you with the grace that clothes your soul; and that this divine presence makes a holy temple, not only of your soul, but also of your body. "Know you not that your bodies are the members of Christ? ... Or know you not, that your members are the temple of the Holy Ghost, who is in you, whom you have from God; and you are not your own?" (1 Cor 6:15,19).

The conscious thought of this divine dwelling — of this incorporation into Christ — has, over the centuries, produced and developed in those docile to the Gospel a religious respect for the body which is expressed in the combination of a person's dress, manners and bearing; in words wisely regulated and measured; expressed, that is, in all modesty. And already, from the beginning of the Church, the Apostle Paul wanted all women to wear a veil to sacred gatherings, and also said to the Corinthians: "You yourselves judge: doth it become a woman, to pray unto God uncovered? ... But if a woman nourish her hair, it is a glory to her; for her hair is given to her for a covering" (1 Cor 11:13,15).

This year, at the head of your thoughts and initiatives, you have written: "the great crusade of purity" — that purity of which modesty is the guardian.

Just as nature places an instinct in every creature, which moves it to defend its life and the integrity of its members; so do conscience and grace (which do not destroy but rather perfect nature), endue the soul with a sense that puts her on vigilant guard — that special characteristic of the young Christian woman — against the dangers which undermine her purity. We read in the *Passio Sanctarum Perpetuae et Felicitatis (Passion of Saints Perpetua and Felicity)* — rightly considered to be one of the most precious gems of ancient Christian literature — that, in the amphitheatre of Carthage, the first concern and gesture of the martyr Vibia Perpetua, when her tunic was rent as she fell in the arena, thrown into the air by a raging bull, was to tidy it in order to cover herself: *pudoris potius memor quam doloris* — "more mindful of modesty than pain".

Fashion and modesty should walk together like two sisters, because both words have the same etymology, from the Latin *modus* — that is, the right measure, beyond which one cannot find the right way. But modesty is no longer in fashion. Similar to those poor alienated people who, having lost the instinct for self-preservation, along with the notion of danger, throw themselves either into the fire or into the river; not a few female souls, made oblivious to Christian modesty by ambitious vanity, woefully face dangers in which their purity may find death. They give in to the tyranny of fashion, even when it is immodest, and in such a way as not even to suspect that it is unbecoming. They have lost the very concept of danger: they have lost the instinct of modesty. Helping these unhappy ones to regain awareness of their duties will be your apostolate, your crusade in the midst of the world. *Modestia vestra nota sit omnibus hominibus* — "Let your modesty be known to all men" (Phil 4:5).

Example

Your apostolate will be, first of all, by example. It will be up to your beloved president and your wise directors to teach you how, before putting on an outfit, you must ask your conscience how Jesus Christ will judge it; and how you must consider, before accepting an invitation, whether your invisible guardian angel will be able to accompany you to such a meeting without veiling his face with his wings; they will tell you which performances, which meeting places, which beaches you should avoid; they will show you how a young woman can be modern, cultured, lively; full of grace, natural elegance and distinction, without bowing to the vulgarities of an unhealthy fashion; preserving a face which ignores artifices (like the soul of which it is the reflection), a gaze without interior or exterior shadows but — at the same time — reserved, sincere and frank.

In the defence of your courageously active purity, We particularly recommend prayer and devotion to the Most Holy Eucharist and to the Blessed and Immaculate Virgin, to whom you are consecrated in a special way. In the Eucharist you find God, who is purity itself, because He is infinite perfection. When He gives Himself to you as — We repeat the words of the prophet — "the corn of the elect, and wine springing forth virgins" (Zach 9:17), Our Lord, "the brightness of eternal light, and the unspotted mirror" (Wis 7:26), purifies your soul and its faculties, your body and its senses. The more a creature approaches God and unites itself with Him, the purer it is; the more it yearns for purity, the more it tends towards Pure Being.

When it pleased the Word to become incarnate and to be born of a woman, He turned His gaze on the most perfect creature: a girl in the grace of her virginity. After adding to this grace the singular miracle of the divine maternity, she appeared of such sublime beauty that artists, poets, and saints have ardently tried, but always in vain, to portray her image. The Church and the angels greet her with the titles of Queen and Mother, whilst those with which the piety of the faithful have encircled her brow, like a diadem of a thousand facets, are innumerable. But among all these titles of glory, there is one which is particularly dear to her and is enough to set her apart: the Virgin! May Mary, this Virgin of virgins, Queen of the Most Holy Rosary, be your model and your strength, throughout your life as young Catholics, and especially in your crusade of purity!

II Address to the Young Women of Catholic Action, 22 May 1941

Crusade against immorality

It is a crusade against those who threaten Christian morality, generated by the peaceful flow of morals among peoples; a crusade against the dangers of powerful waves of immorality, overflowing in the streets of the world and reaching every condition of life.

That such danger is to be found everywhere today is a warning repeated, not only by the Church, but even by men who are outside the Christian faith; the most clear-sighted thinkers, those solicitous for the public good, strongly denounce the sinister threat to the social order and to the future of nations; the poisoning of the roots of life by the present multiplication of incitements to impurity; while the indulgence (which we would do better to call a denial) of an ever-more-extensive part of the public conscience — blind to the most reprehensible moral disorders — slackens the brakes even more.

Is this immorality greater in the present day than in earlier times? It would perhaps be imprudent to say so, and in any case it is an idle question. Already in his day, the author of Ecclesiastes admonished by writing thus: "Say not: What thinkest thou is the cause that former times were better than they are now? for this manner of question is foolish ... All things are hard ... What is it that hath been? the same thing that shall be. What is it that hath been done? the same that shall be done ... Nothing under the sun is new" (Ecc 7:11;1:8–10).

Christian combat

The life of man on earth, even in the Christian era, has always been one of soldiering. We must save our souls and those of the brethren of our time, and the danger has certainly increased today, because ploys designed to excite the passions — confined in other times to small circles — have increased extraordinarily: the progress of the press (cheap publications as well as high-end ones), pictures, illustrations, artistic reproductions (of every shape, colour and price), films, variety shows and a hundred other subtle and secret means, which propagate the enticements of evil and make them available to everyone; to older women as well as to girls. Is there not a daring, indecent fashion before the eyes of every young Christian woman? Does not the cinema now allow one to see spectacles which previously took place behind closed doors, where one would not have dared set foot?

Faced with these dangers, the public authorities in not a few countries have taken legislative and administrative measures aimed at stemming the overflow of immorality. But in the moral field — however praiseworthy, useful and necessary their action may be — it is never sufficient for obtaining those sincere and healthy fruits which heal souls; work which is better suited to higher powers.

The task of Catholic Action

The Church has to work on souls, and Catholic Action, your action, is at her service: in close union with — and under the direction of — the ecclesiastical hierarchy, entering into the fight against the dangers of bad morals, fighting them in all fields open to you: in the field of fashion, clothing and apparel, in the field of personal care and sport, in the field of social relations and entertainment. Your weapons will be your words and your example, your courtesy and your demeanour, which also speak to others and make such behaviour as honours you and your activity both possible and commendable.

It is not Our intention to trace out here the sad and all-too-well-known picture of the disorders which show themselves before your eyes, such as scanty clothes, (which seem to be made to reveal what they should instead veil) sports and exhibitions of "camaraderie" in clothing that is irreconcilable with even the most permissive modesty; dances, shows, auditions, readings, illustrations, decorations in which the mania for fun and pleasure piles up the most serious dangers. Instead, We now intend to remind you and place again before your mind's eye the principles of the Christian faith which, in these matters, must enlighten your judgments, guide your steps and your conduct, inspire and support your spiritual struggle.

Well, it is a struggle! The purity of souls, living in supernatural grace, is never preserved nor will it ever be preserved without a fight. Happy are you, who at the dawn of your life, received in your families a higher, divine life with holy Baptism. Little girls, not conscious of such a great gift and happiness: you did not fight then, as did more mature souls less fortunate than you, for the winning of so much good; but neither will you keep it without a fight. Original sin — although cancelled out in your soul by purifying and sanctifying grace, which has reconciled you to God as adopted daughters and heirs of heaven — left in you that sad inheritance of Adam which is an interior imbalance, a struggle also felt by the great Apostle Paul, who, whilst delighting in the law of God according to the inward man, saw another law of sin existing in his members (Rom 7:22-23); a law of disordered passions and inclinations, never fully submissive — with which an angel of Satan, allied to the flesh and to the world, conspires: harassing souls with temptations.

The war between the spirit and the flesh, so openly attested to by Divine Revelation, is such that — with the exception of the Most Blessed Virgin — any thought of being able to lead a pure life without vigilance and combat is vain. Do not delude yourself into believing that your soul is numb to instigation, invincible to allurements and dangers. It is true that habit often manages to reduce the subjection of the spirit to such disturbances, particularly when it is removed from them and absorbed in great efforts to exercise a higher professional or intellectual activity; but even if one were to imagine all souls, prone as they are to sentimentality, to be capable of rendering themselves immune to the stimuli erupting from images (which, coloured with the balm of pleasure, kidnap and captivate their attention), this would nonetheless be to suppose that the instincts of fallen and disordered human nature can never stop or diminish its malign complicity in those insidious instigations.

The purpose of joint action

You accept this inevitable struggle courageously and in a Christian way. Therefore, the purpose of your joint action cannot be to completely suppress it; but you must strive to ensure that this necessary spiritual battle is not made more difficult, more dangerous for souls, by external circumstances, by the atmosphere in which those hearts which suffer from its assaults must sustain and continue it. In the pugnacious fields of the Church, where virtue and vice face each other, you will always meet some intrepid and heroic characters, moulded by God and supported by grace, who do not waver or collapse at any impulse, and, openly know how to remain uncorrupted and pure in the mud that surrounds them, almost like a leaven of good ferment and of regeneration for more numerous souls who, though redeemed by the Blood of Christ, gather around them.

The aim of your struggle is therefore to make Christian purity (a condition of the salvation of souls) less difficult for everyone of good will; so that temptations arising from external contingencies do not exceed the limits of many souls of mediocre vigour, to whom divine grace gives the strength to fight worthily. To realise such a holy and virtuous intention, it is advisable to act in circles and on lines which — though able to accomplish little or nothing by individual and isolated action — can operate very effectively through joint action. If there is strength in numbers then only a compact group, as large as possible, of resolute and fearless Christian souls will shake off the yoke of certain social conditions, where their conscience demands, and free themselves from the tyranny of all sorts of fashions: fashions in clothing, fashions in the habits and relationships of life. Today more than ever.

Measure is good taste

The fashion movement has nothing bad about it in itself: it springs spontaneously from human sociability, according to the impulse which tends towards harmony with one's fellow men and with the practices of one's own people. God does not ask you to live outside your time, heedless of the needs of fashion, so as to make you ridiculous — dressing opposite to the tastes and customs common to your contemporaries, without ever worrying about what they like.

Whence also, the angelic Saint Thomas affirms, there is no vice in the outward apparel which man uses; but vice comes from the man who uses it immoderately, either in accordance with the custom of those among whom he dwells, or contrary to such custom; by disordered affection for an overabundance of magnificently decorated or pleasing garments, sought-after with excessive attention, whilst humility and simplicity would be sufficiently satisfied with necessary adornment (*Summa Theologiae*, II-II, Q. 169 A.1). And the same holy doctor even goes so far as to say that there can be a meritorious act of virtue in feminine adornment, when it conforms to the manner, measure and good intention of the person; that when women who wear decent clothing — according to their status and dignity and the custom of the country — are moderate in what they do, even their vesture will be an act of that virtue of modesty, which includes the way of walking, acting, dressing and all external movements (cf. Saint Thomas Aquinas, *Commentary on the Prophet Isaias*, end of Chapter III).

Even in conforming to fashion, virtue lies in moderation. What God asks of you is to always remember that fashion is not, nor can it be, the supreme rule of your conduct; that above fashion and its demands, there are higher and more authoritative laws, superior and immutable principles — which can never be sacrificed to the appetite for pleasure or whim — before which the idol of fashion must know how to bend its transient all-powerfulness. These principles have been proclaimed by God, the Church and the saints; by reason and Christian morality; signs of the boundaries beyond which lilies and roses neither sprout nor bloom; and beyond which neither do purity, modesty, decorum and feminine honour spread a cloud of perfumes. There, rather, an unhealthy acrid levity, oblique language, audacious vanity, and the vainglory of the soul, no less than of clothing, breathe and dominate.

These are the principles of feminine adornment that St Thomas Aquinas points to (*Summa Theologiae*, II-II, Q. 169 A. 2) and that he recalls when teaching what the order of our charity and our affections should be (*Summa Theologiae*, II-II, Q. 26 A. 4-5): that we must place the good of the soul before that of the body, and we must prefer the good of our neighbour's soul to our body's good. Do you not see, therefore, that there is a limit that no style of fashion can overstep, beyond which fashion becomes the mother of ruin for one's own soul and for others?

The sacrifices required

Some young women may say that a certain form of dress is more comfortable, and is also more hygenic; but, if it becomes a grave and proximate danger to the health of the soul, it is certainly not healthy for your spirit: you have the duty to give it up. The health of the soul has made heroines and martyrs like Agnes and Cecilia, in the midst of torments and lacerations of their virginal bodies. You, their sisters in faith, in the love of Christ, in the esteem of virtue: will you not find deep in your hearts the courage and strength to sacrifice a little bit of wellbeing, (a physical advantage, if you like) in order to keep the life of your souls safe and pure? And if one's own simple pleasure does not give one the right to endanger the physical health of others, is it not even less legitimate to compromise the health — indeed the very life — of their souls? If, as some claim, a provocative fashion does not leave any bad impression on them, what do they know about the impression that others have? Who assures them that others do not draw evil incitements from it?

You do not know the depths of human frailty, nor the blood of corruption which pours out of the wounds left in human nature by Adam's guilt — ignorance in the intellect, malice in the will, lust for pleasure and weakness towards the passions of the senses — to such a degree that man, pliable as wax to evil, "sees the best and approves it but chooses the worst" (cf. Ovid, Metamorphoses, VII 20) because of that weight, almost leaden, that always drags him down. Oh, how rightly it has been observed that, if some Christians suspected the temptations and falls that they cause in others by their attire and familiarity (to which, in their carelessness, they give so little importance) they would be terrified of their responsibility!

To which We do not hesitate to add: O Christian mothers! If you only knew what future of interior troubles and dangers, of misconceived doubts and badly contained blushes you are preparing for your sons and daughters by the imprudence of letting them become accustomed to being barely covered, of allowing them to lose the candid sense of modesty; you yourselves would blush, and you would fear the dishonour that you do yourselves and the damage you cause the children entrusted to you by Heaven in order to raise them as Christians. And what we say to mothers, we repeat to not a few believing (even pious) women who — by accepting to follow this or that brazen fashion, by their example — cause the final hesitations that prevent a throng of their sisters from rejecting those fashions which could become, for them, a source of spiritual ruin. One dares not wear provocative attire oneself, as long as one is certain that it is the sad preference of women of dubious repute — and the sign, almost, which makes them recognised — but the day it appears on people who are above suspicion, there are no longer any doubts about going with the flow — a flow which may lead to the worst of falls.

Exhortation to enlightened and courageous struggle
It is fitting that all Christian women should have the courage to face such grave moral responsibilities. And you, beloved daughters, out of the lively feeling that you have drawn from

your faith and from the candour of virtue, you have the glory of being united, in your holy crusade as warrioresses of purity. Isolated, your daring would be worth little in opposing the invasion of evil which surrounds you; closely compacted together, however, you will be a legion powerful enough to command respect for the rights of Christian modesty. What is fully acceptable in the fashions, customs and social conveniences that are offered to you; what is only tolerable; what is completely inadmissible, your sense as young Catholics — refined and supported by the wisdom of faith and from the conscious practice of a life of solid piety — will make you see and discern in the light of the Spirit of God and, with the help of His Grace, obtained through prayer, and with the help of the counsels requested of those whom Our Lord has placed at your side as guides and teachers. The clear and deeply felt knowledge of your duty will make you courageous and frank in mutual support in order to accomplish it without hesitation, but with a resolve worthy of your youthful ardour.

Beautiful is the virtue of purity, and sweet is the grace which shines, not only in acts, but also in words, which never oversteps the measure of decorum and courtesy; so that warning and admonition are seasoned with love. And equally shining by grace, before God and men, is the chaste generation which — in our days of trials, sufferings, sacrifices, and austere duties — does not fear to rise with all its power to the heights of the grave responsibilities imposed on it by providence.

Your crusade today, beloved daughters, is not by the sword or blood or martyrdom, but by example, word and exhortation. Against your energies and your intentions, the demon of impurity and of moral licence stands as the principal enemy: lift your heads high to Heaven, whence Christ and His Immaculate Virgin Mother look down on you; be strong and inflexible in fulfilling your duty as a Christian; move against corruption which discourages youth in the defence of purity; render such a service as exceeds all costs to your dear homeland, working effectively and cooperating to spread purity and candour, which can make souls more prudent, more vigilant, more upright, more forceful, more generous.

May the Queen of angels, victrix over the threatening serpent, all pure, all strong in her purity, sustain and direct your efforts in this crusade to which she has inspired you! May she bless your banner and crown it with the pure-white trophies of your victories! We beseech her for this, while in the name of her Divine Son we heartily grant you Our Apostolic Blessing, for you and for all who have united and who will join you in your courageous campaign.

III Letter of the Sacred Congregation of the Council to the Bishops of the Entire World, 15 August 1954

The dangers of immoral fashion
It is a crusade against those who threaten Christian morality, Nobody is unaware that particularly during the summer time, one sees sights, here and there, which cannot fail to offend the eyes and souls of those who have not put aside Christian virtue and human modesty, nor entirely despised them. Not only on beaches and in holiday resorts, but almost everywhere — on the streets of cities and towns, in private and public places and, not infrequently, also in churches — an unworthy and unseemly way of dressing is spreading. There is great danger for the soul of the youth, so inclined to vice, that this abuse will strike a fatal blow to innocence: the most precious and most beautiful ornament of the soul and body. Women's ornamentation, if we can call it ornamentation; women's dress "if we can call 'dress' that which cannot protect the body or modesty" (Seneca, *On Benefits,* VII, 9), sometimes seems to be at the service of shamelessness rather than of modesty.

It has come to the point that everything that happens in private or public life, in terms of depravity and dishonesty, is brazenly published in newspapers and magazines of all kinds, while — in countless cinemas — the same is exposed on-screen for all to see, so that not only callow and unwary youths, but even those of mature age are deeply impressed by these immoral spectacles, so fatal for healthy spirits. Nobody realises what evils derive from them or to what dangers the customs of citizens are exposed. It is therefore necessary, firstly, to put beauty and modesty back in their true light and to recommend it to all; secondly, to repress and prohibit, as far as possible, that which could incite and provoke vice; and finally, with the necessary severity, to lead the world back to good morals. The greatest of the Roman orators said: "We often see men whom nothing would be able to break and make yield to impure suggestions" (Cicero, *Tusculan Disputations*, II, 21).

It is clear that this is a most serious matter, which affects not only Christian virtue, but also the health of the body and the vigour of the development of human society. An ancient poet could rightly affirm: "The nakedness of bodies practised among citizens is the principle of debauchery" (Ennius, *On Cicero, Tusculan Disputations*, IV, 33); therefore, as can easily be seen, this affects not only the Church, but also those in civil government, since they must try to remove that which can weaken and break the strength of the body and the impetus of virtue.

The necessity of the intervention of the bishops

But you, above all, whom "the Holy Ghost hath placed bishops, to rule the church of God" (Acts 20:28), ought to consider this matter carefully, and to cherish and promote, with all your power, everything that contributes to the protection of natural decency and to the advance of Christian morals. "We are all the temple of God, with the Holy Ghost brought and consecrated within us, and the guardian and master of this temple is shame, which will allow nothing unclean or profane to be brought into it, lest God, Who dwells therein, take offence and abandon the polluted house" (Tertullian, *On Female Fashion*, II, 1; Migne, *Patrologia Latina*, I, 1316). As everyone can see from the manner in which women and girls especially clothe themselves today, modesty is gravely offended: modesty "which is the companion of shame, by the presence of which, chastity itself is rendered more secure" (Saint Ambrose, *On The Duties of the Clergy*, II, 69; Migne, *Patrologia Latina*, XVI, 48). Therefore, it is absolutely necessary to exhort all classes of society, and especially the youth, in the way that seems most opportune, to remove themselves from these harmful dangers, which are absolutely contrary to Christian and civic virtues and can expose them to the greatest dangers. "How beautiful is this sense of shame, and how splendid a gem of the moral life!" (Saint Bernard, Sermon LXXXVI, *Sermons on the Canticle of Canticles*; Migne, *Patrologia Latina*, CLXXXIII, 135). Let us be careful not to besmirch and stain it by letting ourselves be carried off by the attractions of vices which arise from fashion, or by the other means of seduction that we have mentioned above, and that no honest person can fail to deplore.

IV Address to the International Congress of Master Tailors, 10 September 1954

Clothing manifests the identity of man

It has often been noted that, among living beings, man is one of the weakest, one of the most in need of natural protection. But God gave man the intelligence that enables him to make up for this deficiency through the exercise of his ingenuity. It is up to you [tailors], therefore, to complete, in a manner of speaking, the work of the Creator, by providing your fellow men with the clothes they need. Christ, making His disciples admire the delicate ornament of a simple wildflower one day, said to them: "Not even Solomon in all his glory was arrayed as one of these" (Mt 6:29). If plants and animals, then, are clothed in wonderful colours which attract the eye and admiration, cannot man imitate the Divine Artist in this?

No doubt he must seek, above all, to defend himself from the elements; but also, to escape the force of habit of daily life, he tries to distinguish himself by accentuating some personal or characteristic trait in the way that he dresses.

On the other hand, clothing sensibly and perennially manifests the condition of the person; it varies according to age, sex and social function; at times, it manifests that which links the individual to a certain social class and that which gives him a special rank, within the same group. Formal dress especially, through richness of materials and impeccable production, seeks to make the excellence of the wearer apparent.

Art and duty of tailors

The materialistic spirit, which inspires so much of civilisation today, has not spared the fashion industry. Too often, a provocative luxury is flaunted, which ignores all modesty and wishes to satisfy vanity and pride.

Clothing, instead of elevating and ennobling, sometimes works to degrade and demean the human person. Even if one is not responsible for these reprehensible displays, one cannot remain indifferent to them. Far from favouring the already-too-pronounced tendency towards immodesty, always be careful to respect the rules of decency and good taste, of a well understood and perfectly honourable elegance. In a word, deliberately put yourself at the service of spiritual aims, rather than following the materialistic current that hauls away so many of your contemporaries. It is not possible to divide human life into sealed compartments, and fix certain lines along which morality might have something to say. Clothing expresses the tendencies and tastes of a person in too instantaneous a way to escape a few very precise rules which surpass and regulate the simply aesthetic point of view.

Though vain ostentation is to be condemned, it is absolutely normal for man to take care to give lustre to the extraordinary circumstances of life with the outward splendour of his clothes, and, in this way, to express his feelings of joy, pride or even sadness. Does not the white dress of a girl on the morning of her First Communion, or that of a young woman on her wedding day, symbolise the exquisitely immaterial magnificence of a soul that offers the best of herself? And furthermore, according to the parable of the Gospel, is entrance into the Kingdom of Heaven not reserved only for those who will be wearing the mysterious wedding garment that God demands of His guests; that is to say, for those with an upright and pure conscience, whose stains have been cancelled out by divine grace, which transforms them and makes them worthy to appear before God?

V Address to the participants of the first International Congress of Haute Couture, 8 November 1957

The problem of female fashion

Beloved sons and daughters, promoters and associates of the Latin Union of Haute Couture, We heartily extend to you Our paternal welcome. You have seen fit to come here and to give Us testimony of your filial devotion and, at the same time, to seek Heaven's favour on your Union. From its very inception you placed it under the auspices of Him whose glory must be the end of every human activity, even of those that are apparently profane, according to the precept of the Apostle of the Gentiles: "Whether you eat or drink, or whatsoever else you do, do all to the glory of God" (1 Cor 10:31).

You propose to examine, from the Christian point of view and with Christian intent, a problem which is both delicate and complex. Its moral aspects cannot be ignored. It is a constant object of attention and anxiety for those whose task it is, by reason of their duties in the family, in society, and in the Church, to preserve souls from the snares of corruption and to protect the whole community from moral decadence: this is the problem of fashion, and of women's fashion especially.

It is right and proper that your generous intentions should receive Our gratitude and that of the Church; and that your Union, born of and inspired by a sound religious and civic conscience, should receive Our fervent wishes for the achievement (through the enlightened self-discipline of designers) of the twofold aim expressed in your statutes: to improve the moral condition of this important sector of public life, and to help raise fashion to the level of an instrument and expression of well-intentioned civility.

Since We wish to encourage such a praiseworthy enterprise, We have willingly consented to your request that We fix Our thoughts on you, particularly in setting out a proper formulation of the problem and, most importantly, of its moral aspects. We shall also make some practical suggestions which may guarantee the Union a well-accepted authority in this highly controversial field.

Three purposes of clothing

Following that counsel of ancient wisdom, which considers the finality of things as the ultimate criterion both for any theoretical evaluation and for the certainty of moral principles, it will be useful to remember those aims that man has always established for himself when having recourse to clothing.

Without doubt, he obeys the familiar requirements of hygiene, decency, and adornment. These are three necessities so deeply rooted in nature that they cannot be disregarded or contradicted without provoking repulsion and prejudice. They are as necessary today as they were yesterday; they are found among virtually every people; they can be seen at every level of the vast scale on which the natural necessity of clothing has manifested, historically and ethnologically. It is important to note the strict interdependence which binds these three necessities, despite the fact that they derive from three different sources. The first is derived from man's physical nature; the second from his spiritual nature; the third from his psychological and artistic nature.

The hygienic requirements of clothing concern mostly the climate and its variations, as well as other external factors which are possible causes of discomfort or illness. It follows from the above-mentioned interdependence that hygienic reasons (or, rather, pretexts) cannot serve to justify a deplorable licence, especially in public, aside from exceptional cases of proven necessity. But even in these cases, every well-bred soul would be unable to avoid the distress of an involuntary feeling of confusion, outwardly expressed by natural blushing.

In the same way, a manner of dressing which is harmful to health — and there are no few examples of this in the history of fashion — cannot be considered legitimate on the pretext of beauty. On the other hand, the common rules of decency must give way to the needs of certain medical treatments which, although it may seem to violate them, actually respects them when all due moral precautions are employed.

Just as obvious as the origin and purpose of clothing is the natural need for decency, which, understood in the broad sense, includes proper consideration for the sensitivity of others to objects that are unsightly and, above all, as a defence of moral honesty and a shield against disordered sensuality.

The strange opinion which attributes the sense of shame to one type of education or another, and even considers it a conceptual deformation of innocent reality — a false product of civilisation, a stimulus to dishonesty, and source of hypocrisy — is not supported by any valid reason. On the contrary, it finds explicit condemnation in the resulting repugnance with which those who dare to adopt this point of view as a way of life are viewed. Thus, the soundness of common sense, manifest in universal usage, is confirmed.

Natural decency, in its strictly moral sense of shame, whatever its origin may be, is founded on the innate and more or less conscious tendency of every person to defend his personal physical good from the indiscriminate desires of others, so that he may reserve it (with prudent choice of circumstances) to those wise purposes which the Creator Himself has placed under the protective cover of chastity and modesty.

This second virtue, modesty (the very word comes from *modus*, a measure or limit) probably better expresses the function of governing and dominating the passions, — especially sensual passions. It is the natural bulwark of chastity; it is its effective rampart, because it moderates those acts which are closely connected with the very object of chastity.

Modesty, like a forward sentinel, makes its warning heard from the moment man acquires the use of reason, even before he learns the full meaning and purpose of chastity. It accompanies him through his entire life and demands that certain acts (which are good in themselves, because they are divinely established) should be protected by a discreet veil of shadow and the reserve of silence, in order to confer on them the respect owed to the dignity of their great purpose.

It is therefore just that modesty, as the depository of such precious possessions, should claim for itself an authority prevailing over every other tendency and every caprice, and should preside over the determination of manners of dressing.

The third purpose of clothing, from which fashion originates more directly, responds to the innate need — more acutely felt by woman — to enhance the beauty and dignity of the person by the same means that are suitable to satisfy the other two purposes. The term "adornment" is preferable to "beautification" in order to avoid restricting the scope of this third requirement to mere physical beauty, and, all the more, to avoid reducing the phenomenon of fashion to the purpose of seduction as its first and only cause. This penchant for the adornment of one's person clearly derives from nature, and is therefore legitimate.

Over and above that function of clothing which hides physical imperfections, youth demands attractive and splendid clothing which sing the happy themes of the springtime of life, and which facilitates, in harmony with the rules of modesty, the psychological prerequisites necessary for the formation of new families. At the same time, those of mature age seek appropriate clothing to enhance an aura of dignity, seriousness and serene happiness. In those cases where the aim is to enhance the moral beauty of the person, the style of clothes will be such as almost to eclipse physical beauty in the austere shadow of concealment, in order to distract the attention of the senses, and concentrate reflection on the spirit.

Considered under this wider aspect, clothing has its own multiform and efficacious language. At times, it is a spontaneous and faithful interpretation of sentiments and habits; at other times, it is conventional, affected and, therefore, hardly sincere. Clothing expresses joy and sorrow, authority and power, pride and simplicity, wealth and poverty, the sacred and the profane. The specific form of this expression depends on the traditions and culture of a particular people; the stabler the institutions, characters, and sentiments that fashion interprets, the slower clothing changes.

The characteristics of fashion

Fashion — an ancient art of uncertain origin, which is made complex by the psychological and social factors it involves — applies itself expressly to the enhancement of physical beauty. At present, fashion has gained an indisputable importance in public life, whether as an aesthetic expression of custom, or as an interpretation of public demand and a focal point of substantial economic interests.

A thorough observation of the phenomena of fashion will reveal that they are not only extravagant in their form, but are also the meeting point of different psychological and moral factors — such as the taste for beauty, the thirst for novelty, the affirmation of personality, the intolerance of monotony — no less than of luxury, ambition and vanity.

Fashion is actually elegance; conditioned, however, by continuous change, in such a way that its own instability confers on it its most distinctive mark. The reason for its constant (now seasonal) change — slower along its essential lines, but extremely rapid in its accidental variations — seems to be found in an anxiety to overcome the past, facilitated by the frantic character of the present era, which has the tremendous power to quickly burn through everything which is intended for the satisfaction of the imagination and the senses. It is understandable that new generations, intent on their own future — dreaming of a different and better life than that of their fathers — should feel the need to detach themselves, not only from those forms of clothing, but also of objects and ornaments, which most obviously recall a way of life that they wish to surpass. But the extreme instability of present-day styles is determined, above all, by the will of its creators and guides, who have at their disposal means unknown in the past, such as enormous and varied textile production, the inventive fertility of designers, and easy means of launching fashions in the press and in movies, television, exhibitions, and fashion shows. The rapidity of change is further stimulated by a kind of silent competition (in truth, not new) between the "elite" who wish to assert their own personality by original forms of clothing, and the public which immediately appropriates them for its own use by more or less felicitous imitations. Nor can one overlook another subtle and decadent reason; namely, the effort of those designers who play on the factor of seduction in order to ensure the success of their creations, being well aware of the effect of constantly renewed surprise and novelty.

Another characteristic of today's fashion is that, while remaining principally aesthetic, it has also, in large proportion, taken on economic properties. The few established haute-couture tailors, which once dictated, from this or that metropolis, the undisputed rules of elegance to the world of European culture, have now been replaced by a number of financially powerful organisations which, while supplying the demand for clothing, also form popular tastes and constantly work to promote increasing demands for their own market. The reasons for this transformation are to be found, first of all, in the so-called "democratisation" of fashion, through which an increasing number of individuals fall under the spell of elegance and, secondly, in technical progress which makes it possible to turn out mass-produced styles which would once have been expensive but have now become easy to obtain cheaply and "ready-tailored" on the market. Thus the world of fashion was born: a world which includes artists and craftsmen, manufacturers and merchants, publishers and critics, as well as an entire class of humble workers who earn their living from fashion.

Although economic factors are the driving force of this activity, its soul is always the designer: the person who, through an ingenious choice of materials, colours, cut, line, and ornaments, gives life to a new and expressive style appreciated by the public. This is to say nothing of the difficulties of his art, the fruit of genius and skill and, moreover, of a certain sensitivity to the taste of the moment. A design certain of success acquires the importance of an invention. It is surrounded by secrecy while awaiting its "launch". Once on the market, it fetches a high price, and the media give it wide publicity, almost as if it were an event of national interest. The influence of designers is so strong that the textile industry lets its production be guided by them, both in quantity and in quality. Just as great is their social influence in interpreting public customs — for if fashion has been the external expression of the usages of people in the past, in times when this phenomenon took place as a result of reflection and study, then it has become even more so today.

But the formation of the tastes and preferences of the people and the guidance of society toward serious or decadent habits do not depend on the fashion designers alone. It depends also on the whole organised complex of the industry, especially on fashion houses and critics in that more refined sector which finds its clients in the upper social classes and takes the name of *haute couture*, as if to designate the source of the currents that people will later follow, almost blindly, under what appears to be some magic compulsion.

Now, since so many important values are involved in and sometimes endangered by fashion, as We have briefly outlined, it seems providential that there should enter upon the scene persons who have received a technical and Christian formation and want to help free fashion from those tendencies which are not commendable.

These are persons who see in styles the art of knowing how to dress, whose aim is certainly (although only partially) to enhance the beauty of the body, but with such moderation that the body — the masterpiece of divine creation — will not be obscured but, on the contrary, in the words of the Prince of the Apostles, will be exalted "in the incorruptibility of a quiet and a meek spirit, which is rich in the sight of God" (1 Peter 3:4).

Honest and dishonest fashion

The problem of fashion consists in the harmonious reconciliation of a person's exterior ornamentation with the interior of a quiet and modest spirit. However, some people ask themselves if there really is a moral problem in something as superficial, contingent, and relative as fashion. And, granted that there is, they ask in what terms this problem is to be set forth and according to what principles it must be solved.

This is not the place to protest at length against the insistent attempts of many contemporaries to separate the exterior activities of man from the moral realm as if the two belonged to different universes, as if man himself were neither the subject nor the object of the moral realm, nor therefore responsible before the Sovereign Regulator of all things. It is quite true that fashion is like art, science, politics, and other so-called profane activities, which follow their own rules to attain the immediate ends for which they are intended. Their subject, however, is invariably man, who cannot prescind from directing these activities to his ultimate and supreme end.

The moral problem of fashion exists, then, not only insofar as it concerns a generically human activity but, more specifically, insofar as this activity is carried out in a field common to, or at least very close to, obvious moral values. The problem is especially grave insofar as the aims of fashion (which are good in themselves) are likely to be twisted by the wicked tendencies of human nature, fallen through original sin. Thus, fashions can be changed into occasions of sin and scandal. This inclination of corrupt human nature to abuse fashions has frequently led ecclesiastical tradition to treat them with suspicion and severe judgment, as expressed with intense firmness by notable sacred speakers and zealous missionaries, even to the point of burning vain objects: an action esteemed by the people, according to the usages and austerity of the day, as effective eloquence.

One cannot argue, from these manifestations of severity, which demonstrated, above all, the maternal concern of the Church for the welfare of souls and the moral values of civilisation, that Christianity exacts a near-renunciation of respect and care for the physical person and its external decorum. To draw this conclusion would be to forget what the Apostle of the Gentiles wrote: "I will therefore ... women also in decent apparel: adorning themselves with modesty and sobriety" (1 Tim 2:8,9).

On the contrary, the Church does not censure or condemn fashion when it is meant for the proper decorum and ornamentation of the body, but she never fails to warn the faithful against being easily led astray by it.

This positive attitude of the Church derives from reasons far higher than the mere aesthetic or hedonistic considerations that have been assumed by a reinvigorated paganism. The Church knows and teaches that the human body, which is God's masterpiece in the visible world, and which has been placed at the service of the soul, has been elevated by the Divine Redeemer to the rank of temple and instrument of the Holy Ghost, and as such, must be respected. The body's beauty must therefore not be exalted as an end in itself; much less, so as to demean the dignity bestowed on it.

Speaking in concrete terms, it cannot be denied that, along with seemly fashions, there are also immodest ones that create confusion in well-ordered minds and can even be an incentive to evil. It is always difficult to indicate the line between seemliness and shamelessness by universal norms, because the moral evaluation of attire depends on many factors. However, the so-called relativity of fashions with respect to times, places, persons, and education is not a valid reason to renounce *a priori* a moral judgment on this or that fashion which, for the time being, violates the limits of normal decency. The sense of shame, almost without being consulted on the matter, gives immediate warning as to where immodesty and seduction, idolatry of matter and luxury (or simple frivolity) might be lurking. And if the creators of shameless fashions are skilled in the trafficking of perversion, mixing it into an ensemble of aesthetic elements that are good in themselves, human sensuality is unfortunately even more skilful in discovering it and is ready to fall under its spell. Here as elsewhere, greater sensitivity to this warning against the snares of evil, far from being grounds for criticising those who possess it, as though it were a sign of interior depravity, is actually a mark of the upright soul and of watchfulness over the passions. Yet, however broad and changeable the relative morals of styles may be, there is always an absolute norm to be kept, after having heard the admonitions of conscience, which warns against approaching danger: style must never be a proximate occasion of sin.

Among the objective elements which concur to make an immodest design, there is, first and foremost, the evil intention of its makers. When these seek to create unchaste ideas and sensations through their fashions, then a machination of disguised malice is present. They know, among other things, that boldness in such matters cannot be pushed beyond certain limits, but they also know that the desired effect is near these limits, and that a clever combination of serious and artistic elements with other, less worthy elements is highly suited to capturing the fancy and the senses. For they realise that a fashion thus devised will be acceptable to a client who seeks such an effect, without compromising, at least in their opinion, the good name of honest people. Every restoration of fashion must therefore begin with the intention of the designer and of the wearer. In both, there must be an awakening of the conscience as to their responsibility for the tragic consequences that could result from clothing which is overly bold, especially if it is worn in public.

More fundamentally, the immorality of some styles depends in great part on excesses either of immodesty or luxury. Practically, an excess of immodesty in a design concerns the cut of the garment. The garment must not be appraised according to the estimation of a decadent or already-corrupt society, but according to the aspirations of a society which prizes the dignity and seriousness of its public attire. It is often said, almost with passive resignation, that fashions reflect the customs of a people. But it would be more exact and much more useful to say that they express the moral direction that a people intends to take: either to be shipwrecked in licentiousness or to maintain itself at the level to which it has been raised by religion and civilisation.

No less unfortunate, although in a different respect, are excesses of fashion when it is assigned the task of satisfying a thirst for luxury. The meagre merit of luxury as a source of labour is almost always nullified by the grave disorders that derive from it in public and private life.

Apart from the squandering of riches that excessive luxury demands of its worshippers — destined for the most part to be devoured by it — it always insults the integrity of those who make a living from their work, whilst also revealing a cynicism toward poverty, either by flaunting too-easy gains or by breeding suspicion about the way of life of those around them. Where moral consciousness does not succeed in moderating the use of riches, even if they are honestly acquired, either frightful barriers will be raised between classes, or the whole of society will be set adrift, exhausted by the race toward a utopia of material happiness.

The principles for solving the moral problem

In indicating the harm that a lack of restraint in styles can do to individuals and society, We do not intend to suggest that the expansive force or the creative genius of designers should be repressed, nor that fashion should be reduced to unchanging forms, to monotony or to dismal severity. On the contrary, We mean to indicate the right road that styles should follow, so that they may achieve their end as faithful interpreters of civilised and Christian traditions. To do this, a few principles may be set out as a basis for solving the moral problem of fashion, from which it is easy to deduce more concrete rules.

The first is not to minimise the importance of fashion's influence for good or evil. The language of clothing, as We have already said, is more effective when it is more ordinary and understood by everyone. It might be said that society speaks through the clothing it wears. Through its clothing, it reveals its secret aspirations and uses it, at least in part, to build or destroy its future. But the Christian, whether he be creator or client, should be careful not to underestimate the dangers and spiritual ruin spread by immodest fashions, because of that continuity which must exist between what one preaches and what one practices. He will remember the great purity which the Redeemer demands of His disciples, even in glances and thoughts. And he will remember the severity which God shows to those who give scandal. We might call to mind on this subject the strong passage of the prophet Isaias, in which was foretold the infamy that was to befall the holy city of Sion because of the immodesty of its daughters (cf. Is 3:16–21); or that of the great Italian poet, whose red-hot words, express his indignation at the immodesty creeping into his city (cf. Dante, *Purgatory*, 23, 94–108).

The second principle is that fashions should be mastered, rather than abandoned to caprice and abjectly served. This applies to the creators of style, designers and critics; conscience demands that they not submit blindly to the depraved taste manifested by society; or rather by a part of it, and not always that part most discerning in wisdom. But it also applies to individuals, whose dignity demands of them that they should liberate themselves with free and enlightened conscience from the imposition of predetermined tastes — especially those debatable on moral grounds. To master fashion also means to react firmly to currents that are contrary to the best traditions. Mastery of fashion does not contradict but rather confirms the saying that "fashions are not born outside of or against society", provided that one ascribes to society, as one should, consciousness and autonomy in directing itself.

The third principle, even more concrete, is due regard for measure, or rather for moderation, in the whole field of fashion. Just as excess is the principal cause of its defects, so will moderation preserve its value. Above all (and at all costs), moderation must provide a pattern for regulating the appetite for luxury, ambition and caprice. Fashion creators, and designers especially, must let themselves be guided by moderation in designing the cut or line of a garment and in choosing its ornaments, convinced that sobriety is the finest quality of art. Far from wanting a return to outdated forms (which not uncommonly reappear as novelties in fashion) but wanting rather to confirm the perennial value of sobriety, We should like to invite today's artists to dwell for a moment on certain feminine figures in the masterpieces of classical art which have undisputed aesthetic value, and where dress, marked by Christian decency, is the worthy ornament of the person with whose beauty it blends as in a single triumph of admirable dignity.

Specific suggestions to promoters and associates of the Latin Union of Haute Couture

Now, beloved sons and daughters, promoters and associates of the Latin Union of Haute Couture. It seems to Us that the word "Latin" itself, with which you have wished to designate your association, expresses not only a geographical region but, above all, the ideal aim of your activity. In fact, this term "Latin", which is so rich in deep significance, seems to express, among other things, a lively sensibility and respect for the values of civilisation and, at the same time, a sense of moderation, of balance and concreteness, all qualities which are necessary to the components of your Union. It has given Us pleasure to see that these characteristics have inspired the purpose of your *Statutes*, which you courteously submitted to Us. We notice that these statutes derive not only from a complete view of the complex problem of fashions, but from your firm persuasion of fashion's moral responsibility. Your programme is, therefore, as wide as the problem itself, since it includes all the determining sectors of fashion — the female sector directly, with the intention of guiding it in the formation of tastes and the choice of clothing; the fashion houses, which are its creators; and the textile industry — so that, by mutual agreement, all might adapt their efforts to the healthy principles of the Union. And since your Union is composed of organisations which are not mere spectators but participants (We might say actors in the theatre of fashions), its program also deals with the economic aspect of fashions, rendered more difficult now by forthcoming changes in production and by the unification of the European markets.

One of the indispensable conditions for achieving the aims of your Union lies in the public formation of sound taste. This is indeed a difficult task, opposed at times by premeditated design, and it requires of you much intelligence, great tact, and patience. Face it with a fearless spirit, in spite of everything. You are certain to find strong allies, first of all, among the excellent Christian families still to be found in great numbers in your native land.

It is clear that your action in this direction must be aimed mainly at winning over to your cause those who control public opinion, through the press and other media. People wish to be guided in style more than in any other activity. Not that they lack a critical sense in matters of aesthetics or propriety, but — at times, too docile and, at other times, too lazy to make use of this faculty — they accept the first thing that is offered to them and only later become aware of how mediocre or unbecoming certain fashions are. It is therefore necessary that your action should be timely. Furthermore, those who enjoy celebrity status, especially in the world of the theatre and film, occupy a pre-eminent position among those who are, at present guiding the tastes of the public most effectively. Just as their responsibility is grave, so will your action be fruitful, if you manage to win at least a few of them for the cause.

A distinguishing mark of your Union seems to lie in the careful study of the aesthetic and moral problems of fashions, conducted in periodic meetings (such as the present congress), which have an ever more international character, persuaded as you are that the fashions of the future will have a unified character on each continent. Strive, therefore, in these conferences, to make the Christian contribution of your own intelligence and expertise; with such persuasive wisdom that no one will be able to suspect you either of personal interest or of compromise. The sound consistency of your principles will be put to the test by the so-called "modern spirit", which cannot bear hindrance. And you will be tested by the indifference of many towards the moral consideration of styles. The most insidious of sophisms are usually repeated to justify immodesty, and appear to be the same everywhere. One of these resurrects the ancient saying, *ab assuetis non fit passio* ("the passions are not aroused by things we are accustomed to") in an attempt to brand as old-fashioned the rebellion of honest people against fashions which are too bold. Is it necessary to demonstrate how out of place this ancient saying is in the present case?

When We spoke of the absolute limits to be defended in the relativism of style, We mentioned the unfounded character of another fallacious opinion, according to which modesty is no longer appropriate in the present era — liberated from all useless and ruinous scruples. It can certainly be conceded that there are different degrees of public morality, according to the times, nature, and conditions of the civilisations of individual peoples. But this does not invalidate the obligation to strive for the ideal of perfection, nor is it a sufficient reason to renounce the high degree of morality that has been achieved, and which manifests itself precisely in the great sensitivity with which consciences regard evil and its snares.

May your Union which aims at ensuring an ever-higher degree of morality in the public customs of your nation, thus have a quick spirit in this battle, and be worthy of its Christian traditions. It is not by chance that We call your work, which strives to moralise fashion, a "battle"; like every other undertaking that intends to restore dominion of the spirit over matter.

Considered individually, they are significant episodes in the bitter and relentless struggle that all must endure in this life who are called to the freedom of the Spirit of God. The Apostle of the Gentiles described the front lines and opposing forces of this combat with inspired accuracy: "For the flesh lusteth against the spirit: and the spirit against the flesh; for these are contrary one to another: so that you do not the things that you would" (Gal 5:17). Thus, enumerating the works of the flesh in an almost bleak inventory of the inheritance of original sin, he also includes impurity among them, to which he opposes modesty as the fruit of the Spirit. Occupy yourselves generously and with confidence, without ever allowing yourselves to be ensnared by that timidity which made the numerically small but heroic armies of the great Judas Maccabeus say: "How shall we, being few, be able to fight against so great a multitude" (1 Mac 3:17). May the same answer given by the great champion of God and of the fatherland encourage you: "For the success of war is not in the multitude of the army, but strength cometh from Heaven" *(Ibid., 19)*.

With this heavenly assurance in mind We take leave of you, beloved sons and daughters. And We raise Our supplications to the Almighty that He might design to bestow His assistance upon your Union, and His graces upon each one of you, upon your families, and, in particular upon the humble working men and women of fashion. As a token of these favours which We wish you, We heartily impart to you Our paternal Apostolic Blessing.

The Teaching of Two Cardinals

Letter of Giuseppe Cardinal Siri to those responsible for Catholic associations and education, 12 June 1960

Concerning men's dress worn by women

This year, the first signs of our late-arriving spring showed a certain increase in the use of men's dress by girls and women; even by mothers of families. Up until 1959, in Genoa, such dress usually meant a person was a tourist, but now there seems to be a significant number of Genoese girls and women who are choosing, at least on excursions, to wear men's dress (men's trousers).

The spread of this behaviour obliges us to give serious consideration to the subject, and we ask those to whom this notification is directed to kindly give this problem all the attention it deserves, as befits those who are aware of being answerable to God.

We seek above all to give a balanced moral judgment upon the wearing of men's dress by women. In fact, our thoughts bear solely upon the moral question

A moral judgment

a) It does not constitute a grave offence to modesty per se

When it comes to the covering of the female body, the wearing of men's trousers by women cannot be said to constitute a grave offence against modesty, because trousers certainly cover more of a woman's body than do modern women's skirts.

b) But it could be one depending on the fitting

Considered from the point of view of fitting, however, it cannot be said that trousers are not sometimes made to fit more tightly than skirts. On the contrary, they are generally of a much closer fitting, such that they may sometimes be of no less concern than exhibition [of the body]. It is therefore a consideration that should not be neglected in the overall judgment, even if it must not be exaggerated.

The gravest aspect

There is, however, another consideration in women wearing men's trousers, which seems to us the most serious. The wearing of men's dress by women:
a) alters the psychology proper to woman;
b) tends to vitiate relationships between women and men;
c) easily harms the dignity of the mother in the eyes of her children.

Each of these points is to be carefully considered in turn.

a) Men's dress changes the psychology of women

In fact, the motive that pushes women to wear men's dress is always that of imitation — nay, of competition with those who are considered stronger, freer, more independent. This motive shows clearly that male dress is the apparent means of bringing about a mental attitude of being "manly". Moreover, since the world began, the clothing a person wears so determines and conditions gestures, attitudes and behaviour, that clothing comes to impose, from the outside, a particular frame of mind.

It should not be ruled out that the wearing of men's dress by women conceals, to a greater or lesser extent, her response to her own femininity, which appears to her to be inferiority when, in fact, it is only difference. The perversion of her psychology becomes evident.

These reasons, whilst there are many others, are sufficient to alert us to how the mentality of women becomes deformed by the wearing of male dress.

b) Male dress tends to vitiate relationships between women and men

In fact, relationships between the sexes, when they blossom with the coming of age, are dominated by an instinct of mutual attraction. The essential basis of this attraction are those differences between the sexes which are all that makes complementarity possible. If these differences are made less evident by the elimination of their external signs and the stifling of their normal psychological conformation, it results in a fundamental element in the relationship being altered.

That is not all, however; attraction is naturally preceded, chronologically, by that sense of shame which restrains, imposes respect and tends towards lifting up to a higher level of mutual esteem and healthy fear those impulses which would otherwise give rise to less controlled acts. To transform clothing which, in its difference, would set boundaries and encourage resistance, tends, instead, by removing distinctions, to break down the protection provided by the sense of shame. It, at least, impedes it. Without the restraints of the sense of shame, relationships between man and woman are prone to degrade into pure sensuality, without respect or esteem.

Experience tells us that when woman becomes like a man, defences are impaired and weakness increases.

c) Male dress harms the dignity of the mother
All children instinctively have a sense of their mother's dignity and decorum. Analysis of the inner crisis which children experience when they awaken to life around them — even before adolescence — reveals how important is the sense of the mother in the life of a child. Children are very delicate on this point. Adults, in general, have forgotten all this and have lost their sense of it. We would do well to reconsider the immense instinctive needs of children for their mother, and the deep and even terrible reactions roused by discoveries of their mother's misbehaviour. Many traits in later life are sketched out — and for ill — in these first innermost events of infancy and childhood.

A child does not know the definitions of exhibition, frivolity or infidelity, but has an intuition of these things, and an instinct to suffer and to be bitterly wounded by them in his soul.

In the long run, this practice is macerating the human order

Even if one acknowledges that a woman's appearance in men's dress may not immediately give rise to the same disturbance as grave immodesty, let us reflect carefully about everything said above:

a) Fundamental damage can become irreparable
The alteration of female psychology represents fundamental and, in the long run, irreparable damage to the family, to conjugal fidelity, to the affective sphere and to human coexistence.

It is true that the effects of wearing inappropriate dress are not all to be seen in the short-term. But it is essential to understand that, slowly and insidiously, it has an influence which is undermining, corrosive, and destructive.

b) What may be lost
Is it possible to imagine a satisfying reciprocity between husband and wife if feminine psychology is altered? Is it possible to think of any true education of children — so delicate in its procedure, so interwoven with imponderable factors — in which the mother's intuition and instinct play the most decisive role in those tender years? What will these women be able to give their children when they have worn trousers so long that they think more of competing with men than of being women?

c) The testimony of the human race
Why, since the world began (or rather, since civilisation has been on the move), has there always been an irresistible tendency for everyone to differentiate and divide the functions of the sexes? Is this not perhaps the clear testimony of all mankind to a truth and a law superior to itself?

In conclusion: the question of men's clothing for women must be considered as something which, in the long run, is breaking down human order.

The state of alarm for all those responsible

The logical consequence of everything presented thus far is that a serious and decisive sense of alarm should take hold of all those in positions of responsibility.

a) To form a clear and resolute conscience
We address a grave warning to all parish priests, to priests in general and to confessors in particular; to members of every kind of association, to all men and women religious, especially to teaching sisters.

We invite them to form a clear and resolute conscience on this subject. It is this kind of conscience which matters. It will propose what is needed at the right moment. But it will not let us be resigned, as if we faced something ineluctable; as if we were confronted by the physiological evolution of mankind, etc.

b) The rules of nature and of the eternal law do not change!
Man will come and go as he pleases, because God has left him great liberty of action; but the basic rules of nature and the no-less-substantial rules of eternal law have never changed, are never changing and will never change. There are limits beyond which one may rage as far as one likes, but the result is death; there are limits that can be derided by empty philosophical outpourings, but which constitute the conspiracy of fact and nature against their violators. And history teaches sufficiently, and with terrible evidence in the life of peoples, that the recompense for violating this rule is always catastrophe, sooner or later.

c) Violating the rule of God has dire consequences
Since the Hegelian dialectic, we have heard nothing but fables, and by dint of hearing them repeated, we end up acquiescing to them, if only passively. But the truth is that both nature and truth — and the law which is bound up in both — go on undeterred and crush the naïve who would believe, on no grounds whatsoever, in great and radical changes in human physiognomy itself.

These violations do not lead to a new rule for humanity, but to disorder: harmful instability, the horrendous aridity of souls, the astonishing growth of the waste of humanity; expelled prematurely, left to live out their decline in boredom, sadness and contempt. Broken families, interrupted lives, extinguished hearths, old renegades, degenerate children and, ultimately, despair and suicides — all take root on the ruins of eternal norms. These things attest that the rule of God does not give way and does not admit of any adaptation to the deliriums of so-called philosophers!

How those responsible for souls should act

a) Balance and firmness of principles
We have said that those to whom this notification is addressed are invited to form a clear and resolute conscience about the problem at hand.

Thus they will know what they have to say, starting with little girls in nursery school.

They will know that they have to severely limit their tolerance, in a habitual way, without falling into the errors of exaggeration and fanaticism.

They will know that they must never be so weak as to let it be believed that they are condescending to a practice which is a slippery slope towards undermining morality.

Priests will know that the rule of the confessional must be decisive and strict, even if the use of men's dress [by women] is not to be considered a grave fault in itself.

Everyone will willingly reflect on the need for a rule, reinforced on every side by the contribution of everyone of good will and enlightened mind, so as to create a veritable dam of resistance.

b) Make allies with artisans, journalists and craftsmen
Those responsible for souls, in any capacity, understand how useful it is to have men of art, media and crafts for allies in this defence.

The direction of fashion houses, of their brilliant designers, of the clothing industry is of decisive importance in all this. The confluence of the sense of art, refinement and good taste can find convenient but worthy solutions as to the dress of women who have to use a motorcycle or engage in certain work or exercise. The important thing is to preserve modesty together with the eternal sense of femininity, by which — more than anything else — all children will continue to recognise the face of their mother.

c) Contingent experiences must yield to the great values to be saved
There is no denying that modern life poses problems and makes different demands to those of our grandparents. But we affirm that there are values much more in need of saving than incidental experiences, and that — for everyone of intelligence, common sense and good taste — there are acceptable and dignified solutions to problems which arise.

For the sake of charity, we are fighting against that debasement of mankind which is perpetrated by attacking the differences on which the complementarity of the sexes rest.

When one sees a woman in trousers, one must think of her but also of humanity as a whole: of what it will be like when women are masculinised. It is in no-one's interest to promote a future age of the indefinite, the equivocal, the incomplete — and ultimately, of monstrosities.

This letter of ours is not addressed to the public, but to those responsible for souls, for education and for Catholic associations. Let them do their duty, and let them not be caught asleep at the infiltration of evil.

Giuseppe Cardinal Siri,
Archbishop of Genoa

From the writings of Giovanni Cardinal Colombo, 1 June 1971

The shameless display of the female body in the most provocative forms and poses falls into this category of upsetting factors. Licentious fashion constitutes — especially for many men with a still-fragile psychology and still-weaker power of self-control (and these are not found only among young people) — a real aggression towards general stability.

They say: "It's fashionable!" with the same indifference with which one would say: "It's raining!"; as if it were an equally inevitable phenomenon, extraneous to our will. Every one of the faithful must know (and it is our duty as bishop to remember this clearly and firmly) that it is not permissible to remain passive and inert. Something must be done to awaken — first in oneself and then also in others — the dormant sense of the dignity of the body, as an integral and inseparable part of the human person. By degrading the body, the whole man is degraded.

We know that, by reacting against the uncritical conformism to an impudent custom, we run the risk of being greeted with smiles expressing something between irony and pity, as if we were ignoring the relativity of the common sense of shame, and persisted in fighting useless battles, lost at the start. We are convinced that, no matter how relative the common sense of shame is, there nonetheless remain limits beyond which Christian (and even simply human) common sense forbids us to go. Nor do we propose to fight a war against fashion, but only wish to awaken, protect and sustain a conscious, coherent, courageous Christian witness in customs and in life.

Not every style of dress meets the needs of healthy modesty and human dignity. Not every fashion is compatible with the Christian respect due to one's person as a temple of the Holy Ghost (1 Cor 6:19). Not every outfit is suitable for church, where the faithful have the right to find an environment free from the sensual provocations with which the re-paganised city is overflowing. The church must remain a house of God and prayer (Mt 21: 13; Is 56: 7) — a religious place, favourable to the chaste and mystical elevations of the heart.

www.ingramcontent.com/pod-product-compliance
Lightning Source LLC
Chambersburg PA
CBHW030307100526
44590CB00012B/550